ROYAL FAMILIES of the WORLD

By the same author

ROYALTY OF THE WORLD
ELIZABETH OUR QUEEN
THE PRINCE OF WALES
PRINCESS ANNE A GIRL OF OUR TIME
MONARCHY IN POWER
THE PERSIAN PRINCE

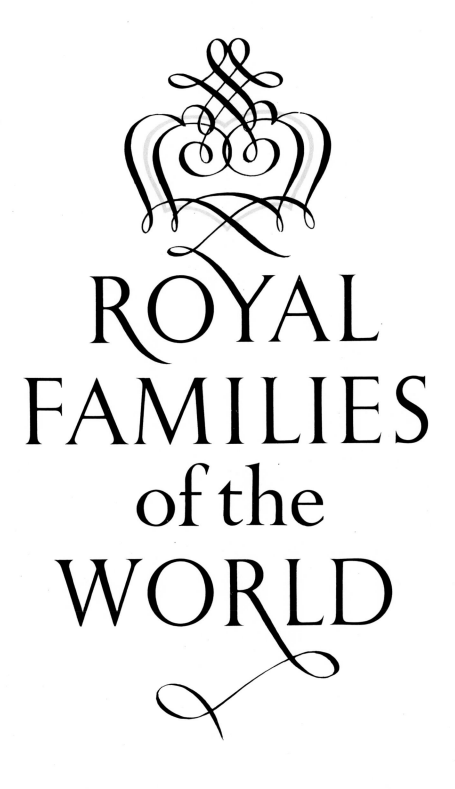

ROYAL
FAMILIES
of the
WORLD

REGINALD DAVIS

COLLINS
St James's Place, London
1978

William Collins Sons & Co Ltd
London · Glasgow · Sydney · Auckland
Toronto · Johannesburg

First published 1978
© Reginald Davis 1978
ISBN 0 00 216717 4

Made and printed in Great Britain by
W S Cowell Limited, Ipswich
Designed by Ron and Karen Bowen

TO MY WIFE AUDREY

ACKNOWLEDGMENTS

Travelling close on two million miles in the taking of royal photographs, I have been privileged to meet most of the royalty of the world. Their courtesy and kindness have made possible some of the finest photographs in my library of 27,000 colour transparencies and I should like to take this opportunity of expressing my sincere thanks to the Royal Families who have helped make this book possible. My grateful thanks also to those members of their Households whose kindness, co-operation and assistance has contributed so much to the success of my work.

Finally, my thanks to Princess Anne-Lise of Schaumberg-Lippe, of Denmark; Ernst G. Mortensens Forlag, and Arne Knudsen of Norway.

CONTENTS

Queen Victoria
Prince Albert
of Saxe-Coburg-Gotha

Princess Victoria Adelaide
Kaiser Frederick III
of Germany

King Edward VII
Princess Alexandra
of Denmark

Princess Sophie
King Constantine I
of Greece

Kaiser William II
Augusta Victoria
of Schleswig-Holstein-
Sonderburg-Augustenburg

Prince Henry
Princess Irene
of Hesse

**Prince
Albert Victor**

King George V
Princess Mary
of Teck

Princess Louise
Duke of Fife

Princess Victoria

Princess Maud
King Haakon VII
of Norway

**Prince
Alexander**

**Prince
William**
Princess
Cecilie

**Prince
Frederick**

**Prince
Adalbert**

**Prince
August William**

**Prince
Oscar**

**Prince
Joachim**

**Duchess
Victoria Louise**

Alexandra   Maud

**Prince
Louis Ferdinand**
Princess Kira

King Edward VIII

**Princess Royal
Mary**
Viscount Lascelles

**Prince Henry
Duke of
Gloucester**
Lady Alice Scott

Prince John

**King George II
of Greece**
Princess Elizabeth
of Romania

Princess Elaine
King Carol
of Romania

Princess Irene
Duke of Aosta

King George VI
Lady Elizabeth
Bowes-Lyon

**Prince George
Duke of Kent**
Princess Marina
of Greece

**King Olav V
of Norway**
Princess Martha
of Sweden

**King Alexander I
of Greece**
Aspasia-Manou

**King Paul I
of Greece**
Frederica
of Hanover

**Princess
Katherine**

**Hon. Gerald David
Lascelles**

**Princess
Alexandra**

**Michael of
Romania**

Duke of Aosta

George Henry Hubert
Earl of Harewood

Prince William

**Prince Richard
Duke of
Gloucester**
Birgitte van Deurs

**Princess
Ragnhild**

**Princess
Astrid**

Prince Harald
Sonja Haraldson

Princess Sophia
Juan Carlos
of Spain (King)

Princess Irene

**King Constantine II
of Greece**
Princess Anne-Marie
of Denmark

Queen Elizabeth II
Prince Philip
of Greece

Princess Margaret
Anthony
Armstrong-Jones

**Prince Edward
Duke of Kent**
Katherine
Worsley

Princess Alexandra
Hon Angus Ogilvy

Prince Michael
Baroness
Marie-Christine
von Reibnitz

**Princess
Alexia**

**Prince
Paul**

**Prince
Nicolaos**

**David
Viscount Linley**

**Lady Sarah
Armstrong-Jones**

Marina Victoria   James

Martha   Haakon

**Princess
Elena**

**Princess
Cristina**

**Prince
Felippe**

Prince Charles

Prince Andrew

Prince Edward

**Lady Helen
Windsor**

Princess Anne
Mark Phillips

**George
Earl St Andrews**

Peter

Prince Alfred
Duchess Marie
of Russia

Princess Louise
Duke of Argyll

Prince Leopold
Helen
of Waldeck

Princess Alice
Prince Louis
of Hesse-Darmstadt

Princess Helena
Prince Christian of
Schleswig-Holstein

Prince Arthur
Princess Louise
of Prussia

Princess Beatrice
Prince Henry
of Battenberg

Princess Alice

Princess Elizabeth
Grand Duke Serge
of Russia

**Alexander
Marquis of
Carisbrooke**

Victoria Ena
King Alfonsa XIII
of Spain

Leopold

Maurice

Princess Victoria
Prince Louis
of Battenberg

Princess Alix
Tsar Nicholas II
of Russia

**Princess Alice
of Battenberg**
Prince Andrew
of Greece

Lord Louis Mountbatten
Edwina Ashley

Prince Philip

Patricia Edwina

Pamela

UNITED
KINGDOM
The House of Windsor

QUEEN ELIZABETH II
The House of Windsor

Elizabeth II, 'by the Grace of God, of the United Kingdom of Great Britain and Northern Ireland and of her other realms and territories, Queen, Head of the Commonwealth, Defender of the Faith . . .' proud titles borne by a queen directly descended from Egbert King of Wessex who died in 839. He was called Bretwalda, Ruler of Britain.

Down the years, titles were added and subtracted, one of the most illustrious being Empress of India, accorded to Victoria. The title of Emperor continued with her son, grandson, and great grandson, but was no longer pertinent to George VI. A wise, gentle, dedicated king, he gave Britain her second Elizabeth.

The first child of the Duke and Duchess of York, she was born at 17 Bruton Street, London, on 21st April 1926, and christened Elizabeth Alexandra Mary in the chapel at Buckingham Palace. The family soon moved to 145 Piccadilly, and much of her childhood was divided between London, the White Lodge in Richmond Park, and the country homes of her grandparents.

Princess Margaret was born on 21st August 1930.

When the Duke of York succeeded to the throne on 11th December 1936, Princess Elizabeth became heiress presumptive. At eighteen, she was appointed a Counsellor of state while her father toured the Italian battlefields, and in July 1944 the King granted her armorial bearings.

In 1947 the Princess accompanied her parents and sister on a tour of South Africa; soon afterwards the King announced her engagement to Lieutenant Philip Mountbatten. Born Prince Philip of Greece, only son of the late Prince Andrew of Greece and Denmark, and Princess Alice, daughter of the 1st Marquess of Milford Haven, he renounced his title when he became a British subject. Through his mother he is a great-great-grandson of Queen Victoria as Elizabeth, through her father, is a great-great-granddaughter.

They were married on 20th November 1947. On the eve of their wedding the King created Lt. Mountbatten Duke of Edinburgh, Earl of Merioneth and Baron Greenwich, and a Knight of the Garter, with the title of His Royal Highness. Prince Charles was born the following year on 14th November, Princess Anne on 15th August 1950, Prince Andrew on 19th February 1960 and Prince Edward on 10th March 1964.

The Duke continued his naval career until, in 1951, it was announced he would take up no further naval engagements until the King and Queen returned from their proposed Commonwealth tour.

When the King's illness prevented the tour, the Princess and the Duke went instead, and in Kenya the Princess received news of her father's death. She was crowned Queen in Westminster Abbey on 2nd June 1953.

The Duke assumed an increasingly important role in the country's affairs, and in 1957 the Queen granted him the style and dignity of a Prince of the United Kingdom. His driving enthusiasm and tireless activities have taken him all over the world.

He has accepted presidencies of a wide range of organisations; he is Grand Master of the Guild of Air Pilots and Air Navigators of the British Empire. He rides, has played cricket and is a past president of the MCC; he sails and is Admiral of the Royal Yacht Squadron.

Between them, the Queen and Prince Philip cover almost every facet of life today. Not least important is their own family circle. Princess Anne married Captain Mark Phillips in November 1973. Four years later their son, Peter Mark Andrew was born; he is the Queen's first grandchild and the first royal baby to be born a commoner for five hundred years. He will be known to the world as plain Master Phillips. Prince Charles has served in both the Royal Navy and the Royal Air Force and now undertakes numerous public duties in his own right and on his mother's behalf. As he approaches his thirtieth birthday he will be finding that more and more of the duties of royalty will fall on his shoulders. His younger brothers Prince Andrew and Prince Edward are both growing up fast, Edward at the threshold of a career at Gordonstoun where his brothers and his father were at school.

Had the Queen not succeeded to the throne, she would probably have followed country pursuits. But even before she was crowned, she had dedicated herself to her people in a twenty-first birthday broadcast from Cape Town:

'I declare before you all that my whole life, whether it be long or short, shall be devoted to your service and the service of our great imperial family to which we all belong. . . . God help me to make good my vow, and God bless all of you who are willing to share it.'

In 1977 the Queen celebrated the Silver Jubilee of her reign. The demonstrations of enthusiasm that greeted the event, every bit as fervent as those expressed at Queen Victoria's Diamond Jubilee in 1897, are as clear an indication as any that in the eyes of her people these promises have been fulfilled in the spirit as well as the letter by the second Queen Elizabeth.

Her Majesty Queen Elizabeth II in the Mantle and
Insignia of the most noble order of chivalry in the
world, the Order of the Garter, in procession to
St George's Chapel, Windsor, for the annual
thanksgiving service.

Opposite Queen Elizabeth II with the Duke of Edinburgh, driving in the Irish State Coach to open Parliament.

Left In the full dress uniform and wearing the plume of the Grenadier Guards the Queen, accompanied by the Duke of Edinburgh, leaves Buckingham Palace for the Sovereign's Birthday Parade of Trooping the Colour.

Below The glittering coronation coach carrying the Queen about to leave Buckingham Palace for St Paul's Cathedral for the Thanksgiving Service on Her Majesty's Silver Jubilee, 7th June, 1977.

Left Queen Elizabeth II with President Gerald Ford at the British Embassy in Washington during the state visit to the United States in 1976.

Below The Royal Opera House, Covent Garden, at the Première of Rossini's 'La Cenerentola' by the opera company of La Scala, in 1976. Queen Elizabeth II is with Madame Vittoria Leone, wife of the President of Italy.

Top Spectacular in her scarlet robe, the Queen descends the steps of St Paul's Cathedral following a service of thanksgiving for the Order of the British Empire.

Middle Queen Elizabeth II accompanied by the President, Mr Gerald Ford, inspects the Guard of Honour on the lawn of the White House during her state visit to the United States in 1976.

Bottom Queen Elizabeth II at the Maundy Service, Westminster, 1973 – escorted by the Dean.

Right Queen Elizabeth the Queen Mother.

Far right In brilliant sunshine the Queen Mother followed by Princess Margaret and Princess Alexandra at the Royal Meeting, Ascot.

Bottom right Queen Elizabeth with her mother at the Badminton Horse Trials.

Below Members of the Royal Family watching the cross-country event at the Badminton Horse Trials. Lady Sarah Armstrong-Jones takes photographs while Princess Margaret, Elizabeth the Queen Mother, the Duke of Beaufort and the Queen look on.

Right At the Badminton Horse Trials in 1976 Prince Charles sports a beard for the first time in public as he takes a ride with Sir John Miller.

Opposite The Prince of Wales at Yeovilton Naval Air Base as he leaves the operations room to join his helicopter, 1974.

Below Prince Charles smoking a pipe of peace as he is made an Indian Chief of the Kainai Tribe with the name of 'Red Crow' in Alberta, Canada, 1977.

Previous spread Princess
Anne and Captain Mark
Phillips with members of
the Royal Family
acknowledge the cheers
of the crowds from the
balcony of Buckingham
Palace after their wedding
in Westminster Abbey on
14th November, 1973.

Opposite left In an open landau Princess Anne and Captain Mark Phillips leave Buckingham Palace for St Paul's Cathedral to attend the Thanksgiving Service on the Queen's Silver Jubilee, 7th June, 1977.

Opposite lower left The christening of baby Peter at Buckingham Palace. Princess Anne holds her son amid all the excitement on his first public appearance.

Opposite lower right A relaxed moment at Persepolis, Iran 1971. One of my favourite pictures of Princess Anne.

Right Princess Anne allows herself a moment for reflection before the most skilled and elegant of all equestrian events – the dressage.

Below Princess Anne in action on Goodwill at Kiev, Russia during the World Championship Three Day Event, 1973.

Above David, Viscount Linley with his cousin Prince Edward as they watch the Cross-country Event at the Badminton Horse Trials, 1976.

Left Prince Andrew in a joyful mood as he watches the Calgary Stampede in Alberta, Canada in 1977.

Left Queen Elizabeth II at the Royal Festival Hall.

Below Queen Elizabeth II during her state visit to the United States is seen at the University of Virginia as she walks among the crowds and receives a bouquet from a watching admirer.

King George IV
of Great Britain
Caroline of Brunswick

Princess Charlotte
Prince Leopold
of Saxe-Coburg-Gotha
(King Leopold I of Belgium)
later married
Princess Louise d'Orleans

King Leopold II
Marie Archduchess of Austria

Philippe Comte de Flandre
Princess Marie
of Hohenzollern-Sigmaringen

Princess Charlotte
Archduke Maximilian
Emperor of Mexico

Prince Leopold
Comte de Hainaut

Princess Louise

Princess Stephanie
Prince Rudolph
of Austria

Princess Clementine

Prince Baudouin

Princess Henriette

Princess Josephine

King Albert I
Princess Elizabeth
of Bavaria

King Leopold III

Prince Charles Theodore
Comte de Flandre
(Prince Regent 1945–1950)

Princess Marie-Jose
King Umberto of Italy

Princess Astrid
of Sweden

Liliane, Princess de Rethy (2)

Princess Josephine-Charlotte
Grand Duke Jean of Luxembourg

Prince Albert
Donna Paola of Italy

Alexander

Marie-Christine

Marie-Esmeralda

King Baudouin
Dona Fabiola Mora of Spain

Princess Marie Astrid

Prince Henri

Prince Jean

Princess Margaretha

Prince Guillaume

Prince Philippe

Princess Astrid

Prince Laurent

BELGIUM
The House of
Saxe-Coburg Gotha

KING BAUDOUIN
The House of Saxe-Coburg Gotha

His Majesty King Baudouin of the Belgians was born in Brussels on 7th September 1930, with the immediate title of Comte de Hainaut. When his father, Leopold III, succeeded to the throne, he took the title of Duc de Brabant which is reserved for the heir to the throne. The elder son of Leopold and Astrid, Princess of Sweden, Baudouin was five years old when his mother died tragically in a car accident in Switzerland in 1935. He had lived with his brother Albert and sister Princess Josephine-Charlotte, at the Castle of Stuyvenberg in Brussels until King Albert's death in 1934 when the royal family moved to the Palace of Laeken on the outskirts of Brussels where they stayed until the Germans invaded Belgium in 1940. After deliberations with his Ministers, Leopold chose to stay in Belgium, and was taken prisoner by the Germans. In 1941, Leopold married Mademoiselle Mary Liliane Baels. He remained a prisoner at the Palace of Laeken with his children until June 1944, when the entire family was deported to Germany. Before the allied advance, the family were transferred to the Austrian Tyrol from where the 7th American Army liberated them in May 1945. Leopold's brother, Charles, Comte de Flanders, became regent in September 1944 after the liberation of Belgium by Allied Armies, remaining so until 1950.

The King lived quietly in Switzerland until 1950, when he and his children returned to Belgium, where the King asked the government and parliament to vote a law delegating his powers to his eldest son. Ten days later Baudouin became the Prince Royal, and on 17th July 1951, he ascended the throne.

Nine years later on 15th December 1960, he married Dona Fabiola de Mora y Aragon. Fabiola was thirty-two, daughter of the late Don Gonzalo de Mora y Fernandez Riera del Olmo, Conde de Mora, Marques de Casa Riera. She was also charming with a shy serenity and warmth that won the hearts of the not easily pleased Belgian people. She loves music and painting, has travelled widely in Europe and speaks fluent French, Dutch, English, German and Spanish.

They are very happy, their one great sadness – that they have no family of their own. Instead, the Queen devotes an enormous amount of her time to other people's children, to child care and protection, to hospitals, schools and institutions for handicapped children; all the royalties from the French and Dutch versions of her delightful book, *Twelve Wonderful Tales by Queen Fabiola*, were donated to the National Children's Fund.

Both she and the King are very much working monarchs. He begins his day at nine, receiving people in audience in the morning, saving the reading of files and official visits – to universities, factories and museums – because he prefers to keep in touch with his people himself and not through a third person. Fabiola too has broken with tradition. Permanent Ladies-in-Waiting are no longer a part of the royal household, as the Queen, like her husband, prefers personal contact.

Laeken, surrounded by parkland and ornamental lakes, is the royal home. There is a small theatre, a large library of books and records of classical music, and a golf course. An excellent photographer – usually in colour – the King enjoys deep sea fishing and hunts from his lodge in the Ardennes. They have a country house at Opgrimbie near the Dutch border, and it is here, in peace and extreme simplicity, that they enjoy the luxury of a quiet weekend. In 1976 the King celebrated his Silver Jubilee.

Their Majesties King Baudouin and Queen Fabiola at
the Royal Palace in Brussels.

Above An informal Queen Fabiola as she walks among her people in Liège.

Right Queen Fabiola with Princess Sophie (now Queen of Spain) at the Persepolis Celebrations in Iran for the 2,500 years of the Persian dynasty, 1971.

Far right A private talk together as King Baudouin and Queen Fabiola attend the Shah's party at Persepolis.

Opposite Prince Albert and Princess Paola of Liège.

Right The Princess on the balcony of her home.

Below Princess Paola – a lover of animals – seen here on the steps of the Château de Belvedere, Brussels.

Far left Princess Paola playing tennis in Brussels.

Left Prince Phillipe playing tennis indoors in Brussels. In the background is his sister, Princess Astrid.

Below left Princess Paola with her children by the summer house in the garden of her home, the Château de Belvedere in Brussels.

Below The children of Prince Albert and Princess Paola of Liège – Prince Phillipe, Princess Astrid and Prince Laurant.

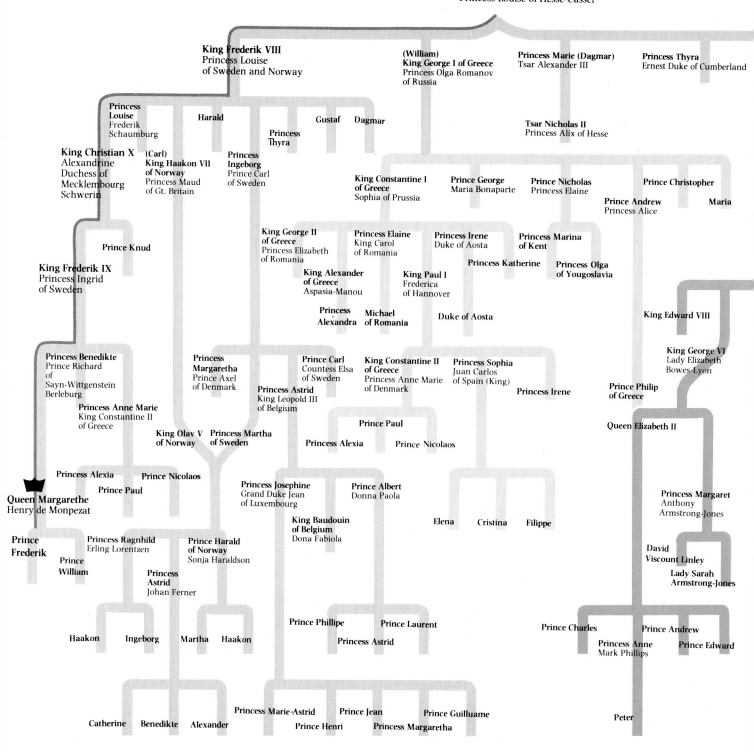

**King Christian IX
of Denmark**
Princess Louise of Hesse-Cassel

King Frederik VIII
Princess Louise
of Sweden and Norway

(William)
King George I of Greece
Princess Olga Romanov
of Russia

Princess Marie (Dagmar)
Tsar Alexander III

Princess Thyra
Ernest Duke of Cumberland

**Princess
Louise**
Frederik
Schaumburg

Harald

Gustaf   Dagmar

**Princess
Thyra**

Tsar Nicholas II
Princess Alix of Hesse

King Christian X
Alexandrine
Duchess of
Mecklembourg
Schwerin

(Carl)
**King Haakon VII
of Norway**
Princess Maud
of Gt. Britain

**Princess
Ingeborg**
Prince Carl
of Sweden

**King Constantine I
of Greece**
Sophia of Prussia

Prince George
Maria Bonaparte

Prince Nicholas
Princess Elaine

Prince Christopher

Prince Andrew
Princess Alice

Maria

Prince Knud

**King George II
of Greece**
Princess Elizabeth
of Romania

Princess Elaine
King Carol
of Romania

Princess Irene
Duke of Aosta

**Princess Marina
of Kent**

King Frederik IX
Princess Ingrid
of Sweden

Princess Katherine

**Princess Olga
of Yougoslavia**

**King Alexander
of Greece**
Aspasia-Manou

King Paul I
Frederica
of Hannover

**Princess
Alexandra**

**Michael
of Romania**

Duke of Aosta

King Edward VIII

Princess Benedikte
Prince Richard
of
Sayn-Wittgenstein
Berleburg

**Princess
Margaretha**
Prince Axel
of Denmark

Prince Carl
Countess Elsa
of Sweden

**King Constantine II
of Greece**
Princess Anne Marie
of Denmark

Princess Sophia
Juan Carlos
of Spain (King)

King George VI
Lady Elizabeth
Bowes-Lyon

Princess Astrid
King Leopold III
of Belgium

Princess Irene

**Prince Philip
of Greece**

Princess Anne Marie
King Constantine II
of Greece

Prince Paul

Queen Elizabeth II

**King Olav V
of Norway**

**Princess Martha
of Sweden**

Princess Alexia

Prince Nicolaos

Princess Alexia   Prince Nicolaos

Princess Josephine
Grand Duke Jean
of Luxembourg

Prince Albert
Donna Paola

Princess Margaret
Anthony
Armstrong-Jones

Prince Paul

Queen Margarethe
Henry de Monpezat

**King Baudouin
of Belgium**
Dona Fabiola

Elena   Cristina   Filippe

David
Viscount Linley

**Prince
Frederik**

Princess Ragnhild
Erling Lorentzen

**Prince Harald
of Norway**
Sonja Haraldson

Lady Sarah
Armstrong-Jones

**Prince
William**

**Princess
Astrid**
Johan Ferner

Prince Phillipe   Prince Laurent

Prince Charles   Prince Andrew

Princess Anne
Mark Phillips

Prince Edward

Haakon   Ingeborg   Martha   Haakon

Princess Astrid

Peter

Catherine   Benedikte   Alexander

Princess Marie-Astrid   Prince Jean   Prince Guilluame

Prince Henri   Princess Margaretha

Prince Waldemar
Marie Dr. of
Duc. de Chartres

Princess Alexandra
King Edward VIII
of Great Britain

Prince Aage

Prince Albert

Princess Louise
Duke of Fife

Princess Maud
King Haakon VII
of Norway

King George V
Princess Mary
of Teck

Princess Victoria

Prince Alexander

Alexandra **Maud**

King Olav V
of Norway

**Princess Royal
(Mary)**
Viscount Lascelles

**Prince Henry
Duke of Gloucester**
Lady Alice Scott

Prince John

See family of
King Frederik VIII

**Hon. Gerald David
Lascelles**

**Prince George
Duke of Kent**
Princess Marina
of Greece

George Henry Huber
Earl of Harewood

**Prince
William**

Prince Richard

Duke of Kent
Katherine Worsley

Princess Alexandra
Hon Angus Ogilvy

Prince Michael

**Lady Helen
Windsor**

James **Marina**

**George
Earl of St. Andrews**

DENMARK
The House of
Sonderborg-Glücksborg

QUEEN MARGRETHE II

House of Sonderborg-Glucksborg

The Danish Royal house is the oldest in Europe and the present sovereign Margrethe II is only the second woman to hold the title of a reigning Queen. The first, also called Margrethe, showed herself to be as capable as any man, her reign spanning the divide between the fourteenth and fifteenth centuries. The monarchy is one noted for its informality and there has been no crowning since the last 'God appointed' absolutist monarch Christian VIII was crowned in 1840.

Queen Margrethe, who succeeded her father Frederik IX in 1972, was born in 1940, one week after the German forces took control of the country. In 1953 she was established as successor to her father by a national referendum and can therefore claim with some justice to have been elected by her people. In 1967 she married Count Henri de Laborde de Monpezat, a French diplomat, who acts as her consort with the title Prince of Denmark.

Queen Margrethe has strong links with Britain. She is known as 'Daisy' after her grandmother Princess Margaret of Connaught and is closely related to both Queen Elizabeth and Prince Philip, the latter being by birth a Prince of Greece and Denmark. She has succeeded her father as Colonel of the Buffs and is a Royal Fellow of the Society of Antiquaries of London. Much of her education took place in Britain as she studied International Law and Archaeology at Cambridge as well as Sociology at the London School of Economics where she is an honorary fellow.

She is one of the most accomplished of European monarchs, with the distinction of having matriculated at no less than five universities. She speaks four languages fluently, is an expert on ju-jitsu and political science as well as having trained in the Danish Women's Royal Air Force. Her main passion is perhaps for archaeology, a taste inherited from King Gustav with whom she spent some time on excavations in Rome. She has also been closely involved with archaeological expeditions in Scandinavia and Egypt. Her father's taste for Classical music has been passed on to her; Sibelius and Beethoven being among her favourite composers.

Prince Henrik shares many of his wife's interests, particularly riding. He is a keen yachtsman and plays tennis most days. As Commissioner of the Danish Red Cross he has a busy week undertaking negotiations and international meetings on their behalf. Modern industry and agriculture are spheres of activity for which he has shown great enthusiasm, on one occasion leading an official Danish export campaign in Saudi Arabia and Iran. His role as consort is by no means always easy, but having the successful example of the Duke of Edinburgh to follow his position has gone from strength to strength. The couple were well prepared for the burdens of monarchy having had five years of married life before Margrethe's succession, throughout which time she acted as regent during her father's frequent absences.

Both the Queen and her husband share a common concern for the happiness and upbringing of their two children Frederik and Joachim. The two little boys lead as normal a life as possible and are in the process of transition from Kindergarten in the Amalienborg Palace to school in Copenhagen. The Queen is often to be found with them watching television or reading stories. The family have an informal cottage outside Copenhagen where they can relax from the cares of office.

Both the Queen and Prince Henrik are aware of the need for flexibility in the monarchy's position. Republicans will not find much cause for rejoicing as a recent poll taken in Denmark showed that 88 per cent of the population is in favour of retaining the monarchy.

Her Majesty Queen Margrethe II with
His Royal Highness Prince Henrik.

Left Kissing Queens as Margrethe welcomes Queen Elizabeth at a return state banquet in London during Queen Margrethe's state visit in 1974.

Below left A happy group at Windsor Castle on a state visit to England in 1974.

Below Queen Margrethe and Prince Henrik in the grounds of the royal palace, Copenhagen.

Left The arrival in an open landau at Windsor Castle with Queen Elizabeth II during a state visit to England in 1974.

Right A wave to onlookers from Queen Margrethe and smiles from Prince Henrik as they leave a banquet in London's Claridge Hotel during their state visit in 1974.

Below At the wedding of Princess Christina of Sweden to Mr Tord Magnusen in June 1974, Queen Ingrid of Denmark sits between Prince Carl Gustaf (now King of Sweden), on her left, and Prince Johann Georg of Hohenzollern. With Prince Carl Gustaf is Princess Margaretha of Sweden and with Prince Johann Georg is his wife, Princess Birgitta.

Opposite Princess Benedikte and Prince Richard in the grounds of their home in Berleburg.

Top right Queen Margrethe with her husband Prince Henrik and their children Frederik and Joachim.

Right Queen Anne-Marie with her husband ex-King Constantine of Greece and their children, Nicolaos, Alexia and Paul, in their home in England.

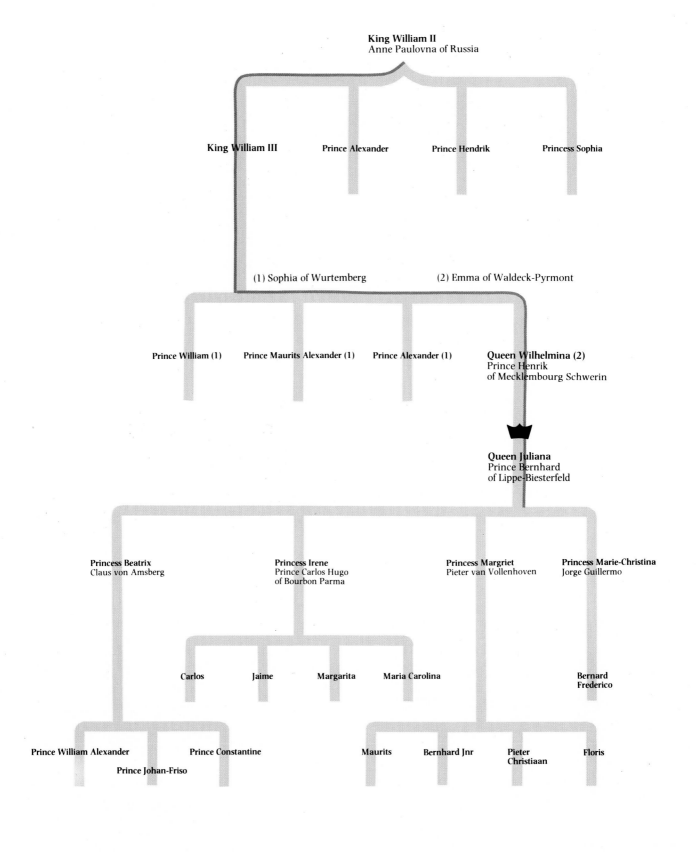

HOLLAND
The House of Orange

QUEEN JULIANA
The House of Orange

The House of Orange-Nassau, to which Queen Juliana of the Netherlands belongs, was created in 1544 through the merging of two great families. The House of Nassau was created in 1159 when a Count Walram of Lauranburg changed his name to Walram of Nassau after the castle in which he lived in Western Germany. Then, in the fifteenth century, the family acquired through marriage large properties in the Netherlands and one of Walram's descendants, William of Nassau, inherited the title of Prince of Orange in 1554 from a cousin, Rene of Chalons.

William, though founder of the House of Orange-Nassau and the Netherlands nation, never actually set foot in his principality, the city of Orange in the south of France. In 1599 he became Statholder or Governor of Holland, Zeeland, and Utrecht for Philip II of Spain who ruled the Low Countries at that time. But dissatisfied with conditions, William led these provinces into rebellion against Spain. He retained his title and became first servant of the new Republic of the United Netherlands. His descendants continued to be Statholders until 1795 when Prince William V fled the country under the French invasion. After the fall of the French Empire in 1815, William V's son was proclaimed William I – the first king of the Netherlands. He was Queen Juliana's great-great-grandfather.

When the male line died out with William III in 1890, his daughter Wilhelmina ascended the throne, her mother Queen Emma acting as Regent during her minority. Wilhelmina, who died in 1963, reigned for fifty years before abdicating in favour of her daughter Juliana, the present Queen, in 1948.

Juliana was born at the Hague on 30th April 1909. In 1937 she married Prince Bernhard von Lippe-Biesterfeld. Their first daughter, Beatrix, 'bringer of happiness', was born a year later; Irene, whose name means 'peace', was born in 1939 a few weeks before the Second World War began. The following year on the 10th May, the Germans invaded and over-ran the country in five bitter days. The royal family escaped to England on a British warship and from there Juliana left with the children for Canada, and it was here that a third daughter Margriet, was born three years later.

From Britain, Queen Wilhelmina headed her government in exile and Prince Bernhard trained as a pilot and was appointed Chief Netherlands Liaison Officer to the Royal Navy, the Army and the Royal Air Force. Later he headed the Netherlands Mission to the British War Office. In 1944 he was appointed Supreme Commander of the Netherlands Army and Air Force, and of the Resistance organizations.

Both the Queen and Princess Juliana returned to Holland in April 1945, shortly before final liberation in May, and relief work began almost immediately.

Princess Christina was born in 1947 and in 1948 Wilhelmina abdicated, Juliana succeeded her and spoke the words that the Dutch people will always remember:

'Who am I that I should be worthy of this?'

But no country was immune from the growing world-wide struggle for independence, and in the second year of the new reign Indonesia became an independent state. Then in February 1953 all Holland was plunged into mourning after the terrible floods in which two thousand people lost their lives.

The Queen is tireless in her concern for her people's welfare. Children, old people, refugees, the sick and the handicapped, she cares for them all. The mother of four former Girl Guides, she gave permission for a Guide Hut to be built in the grounds of the Soestdijk Palace.

Prince Bernhard has played an active part in public life. Since 1976 when his involvement with the Lockheed Company came to light he has resigned most of his offices. Nevertheless, his dynamism and evident desire to continue serving his country will ensure that his role in the future remains important.

Princess Beatrix, heir presumptive to the throne, married Herr Claus von Amsberg, a German diplomat, in March 1966, and they have three sons. Princess Irene, renouncing her right to the throne, married Prince Carlos Hugo of Bourbon Parma in April 1964. Princess Margriet married Peter van Vollenhoven, a law student whom she met while nursing in Leyden Hospital, and Princess Christina is married to Jorge Guillermo.

Her Majesty Queen Juliana.

Below Queen Juliana being
received by Queen Elizabeth in the
Waterloo Chamber of Windsor
Castle during her state visit of
1972. Other members of the
British Royal Family present were
Princess Anne, Princess Margaret,
Lord Snowdon, the Duchess of
Kent, Princess Alexandra and Mr
Angus Ogilvie.

Right His Royal Highness Prince Bernhard.

Bottom right Queen Juliana being received at the Carpenters' Hall in London by the Lord Mayor, Sir Edward Howard, during her state visit to London in 1972.

Below Crown Princess Beatrix and Prince Klaus.

Above Princess Beatrix and Prince
Klaus relaxing with their family.

Previous page Crown Princess
Beatrix and Prince Klaus with
their children in the grounds of
their home, at Drakensteyn
Castle, Utrecht.

Right On a bicycle made for two –
Crown Princess Beatrix and Prince
Klaus enjoying themselves in the
grounds of their home at Utrecht.

Below left Crown Princess Beatrix
with her children William,
Constantine, and Friso.

Below right Princess Irene, Prince
Carlos Hugo and their family
photographed in their home in
Paris.

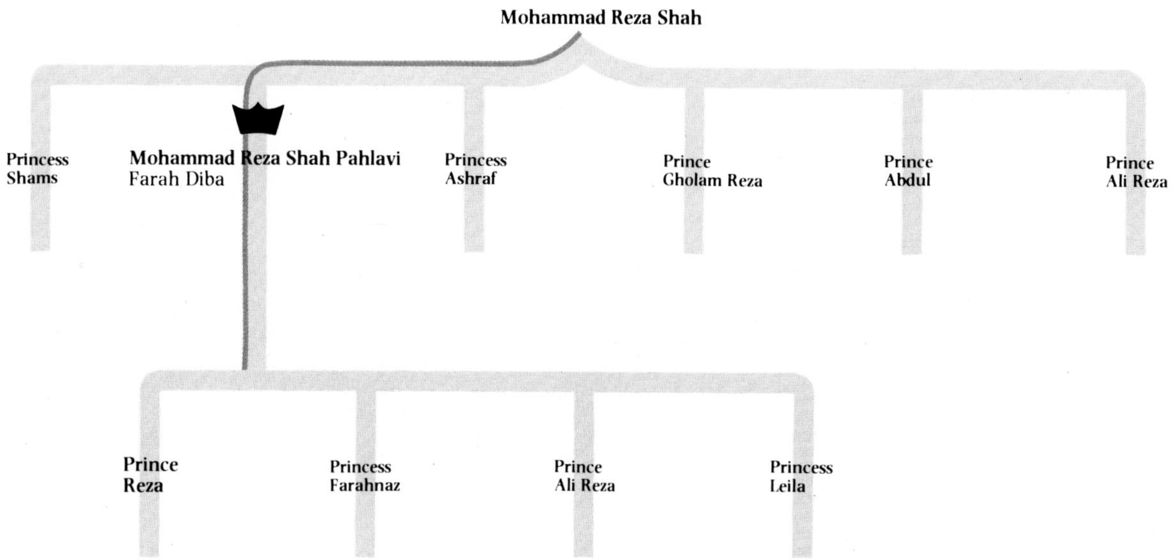

Mohammad Reza Shah

Princess
Shams

Mohammad Reza Shah Pahlavi
Farah Diba

Princess
Ashraf

Prince
Gholam Reza

Prince
Abdul

Prince
Ali Reza

**Prince
Reza**

Princess
Farahnaz

Prince
Ali Reza

Princess
Leila

IRAN
The House of Pahlavi

H.I.M. MOHAMMAD REZA PAHLAVI, ARYAMEHR, SHAHANSHAH

The House of Pahlavi

On 16th September 1979, His Imperial Majesty Mohammad Reza Pahlavi, Shahanshah Aryamehr, will have ruled Iran for thirty-eight years, and in the two thousand five hundred years of his country's monarchy, probably no ruler has been held in greater respect and affection. The Danish orientalist, Christensen, maintained that the ideal King of Iran was not so much the political head of the nation as a teacher and leader. 'He is not only a person who builds roads, bridges, dams and canals, but one who leads them in spirit, thought and heart.' Because the Shahanshah has achieved this, restoring their country from social and economic backwardness to a state of dignity, prosperity and political stability, the people have bestowed upon him the title Aryamehr, Light of the Aryans. It was a token of deep affection and no title he holds is more dear than this.

Born in Teheran on 26th October 1919, he was officially proclaimed Crown Prince on the 25th April 1926, on the coronation of his father the late Reza Shah the Great, a former army officer and founder of the Pahlavi Dynasty. After finishing his schooling in Teheran, the Crown Prince continued his studies in Switzerland, returning to concentrate on military training. He graduated in 1938 and was appointed Inspector of the Iranian Armed Forces.

With World War II Iran proclaimed her neutrality, but on 25th August 1941 Soviet troops from the north and British troops from the south invaded the country. Reza Shah the Great abdicated and on the 16th September the Crown Prince was sworn in as Mohammad Reza Shah Pahlavi, Shahanshah of Iran. He was twenty-two. In 1943 Iran declared war on the Axis powers and in November came the historic conference in Teheran with Churchill, Roosevelt and Stalin.

The years following the end of the war were difficult, with food shortages, inflation and economic chaos, and in 1946 the Shah, by firm handling of the situation, put down a potentially dangerous separatist movement. In accordance with arrangements made by his father, the Shah had married in 1939, Fawzia, sister of Farouk, King of Egypt. She bore him one child only, a daughter, and since the crown constitutionally can only pass to a male heir, the marriage was dissolved in 1948.

The following year, an attempt was made on the Shah's life and although wounded he miraculously survived five pistol shots fired at point blank range.

In 1951 came revolutionary moves towards social and economic reform. The first session of the Senate was inaugurated and a Parliamentary bill signed nationalising the oil industry. The next year the Shah decreed the sale and distribution to farmers of over two thousand villages belonging to the Crown Estates, and in the same year he married Soraya Esfandiari. A European trip was to follow, but a national crisis was developing – the beginning of a struggle for total power by Mossadeq, leader of the National Front and bitter enemy of the Shah.

By the middle of 1953 anarchy reigned, and on 16th August, with shrewdly planned timing, the Shah left on a pilgrimage to the Holy Shi'a Shrines in Iraq. The situation rapidly deteriorated and within three days the whole nation rose against the rebel government. By noon on the 19th the regime was smashed. Three days later the Shah returned to a tumultuous welcome. A new era in the history of Iran had begun.

Steadily reforms instituted by the Shah revolutionised the country's social and economic structure. Feudal systems of land holdings were abolished; women were granted political equality and a well planned, efficiently executed campaign against illiteracy was established.

Health programmes were expanded to extend medical and nursing services to the most isolated villages. A development Corps, of graduates in technology, engineering and agriculture was created to guide and assist villagers towards self help in road building and community affairs; and Houses of Justice were established to enable the poorest people to have recourse to proper judicial settlements of their problems.

But the Shah's problems were not restricted to his public life. Once again his Queen had been unable to bear him a son and he was compelled to divorce Soraya in 1958. In 1959 he met Miss Farah Diba, daughter of an Iranian army officer, and they married that December. As Empress, she has taken a vigorous interest in her country's social welfare, and is as enthusiastic about sport as her husband. Chess is his favourite game. He is a pilot, a voracious reader and an unshakeable believer in God.

On the 31st October 1960, Prince Reza, heir to the throne, was born. Princess Farahnaz Pahlavi was born on 12th March 1963, Prince Ali Reza on the 28th April 1966, and Princess Leila on 27th March 1970.

The Shahanshah in full military uniform with his
Empress in the traditional Iranian colours of
turquoise and white.

Above left The Shah and Crown
Prince, both in full military
uniform, photographed in the
Great Lounge at Niavaran Palace,
Teheran.

Above right The Empress wearing a
cerise evening gown, Iranian style
bodice and white and yellow
diamond tiara – a charming pose
in the Great Lounge at Niavaran
Palace, Teheran.

Opposite Their Imperial Majesties
at Gulistan Palace, Teheran, at the
Saalem ceremony.

Left The Shah and Empress sit on a 1000cc Honda motor cycle in the palace grounds on Kish Island in the Persian Gulf during their *Now Rauz* (New Year) holiday.

Below The Shahanshah riding in the cool of the evening.

Right A very informal picture of the Shah and Empress.

Below right The Iranian Royal family in 1977 at Niavaran Palace, Teheran.

Left Crown Prince Reza fishing in the Persian Gulf.

Top The Crown Prince piloting an F5 fighter aircraft over the Persian Gulf – our wings nearly touched.

Right Crown Prince Reza – a fantastic picture as he rides his 1000cc Honda motor cycle on the island of Kish.

Above The beautiful Empress
Farah.

Opposite A unique royal picture –
the Empress with her children up
a tree on the holiday island of
Kish.

Top right Empress Farah in action
on the ski slopes at Dizin to the
north of Teheran.

Bottom right The Empress scuba-
diving off the coast of Kish, with
her instructors and companions.

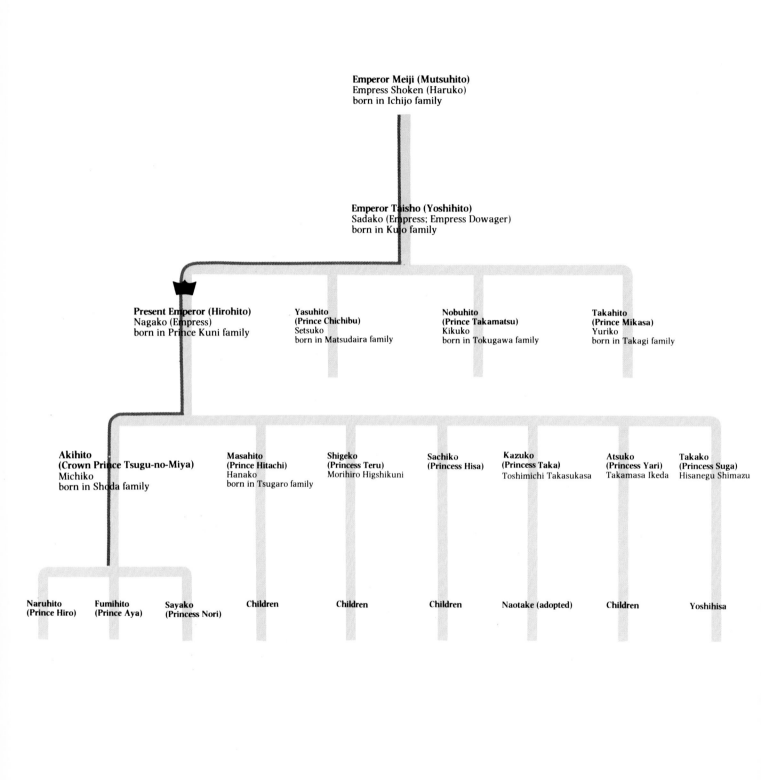

Emperor Meiji (Mutsuhito)
Empress Shoken (Haruko)
born in Ichijo family

Emperor Taisho (Yoshihito)
Sadako (Empress; Empress Dowager)
born in Kujo family

Present Emperor (Hirohito)
Nagako (Empress)
born in Prince Kuni family

**Yasuhito
(Prince Chichibu)**
Setsuko
born in Matsudaira family

**Nobuhito
(Prince Takamatsu)**
Kikuko
born in Tokugawa family

**Takahito
(Prince Mikasa)**
Yuriko
born in Takagi family

**Akihito
(Crown Prince Tsugu-no-Miya)**
Michiko
born in Shoda family

**Masahito
(Prince Hitachi)**
Hanako
born in Tsugaro family

**Shigeko
(Princess Teru)**
Morihiro Higshikuni

**Sachiko
(Princess Hisa)**

**Kazuko
(Princess Taka)**
Toshimichi Takasukasa

**Atsuko
(Princess Yari)**
Takamasa Ikeda

**Takako
(Princess Suga)**
Hisanegu Shimazu

**Naruhito
(Prince Hiro)**

**Fumihito
(Prince Aya)**

**Sayako
(Princess Nori)**

Children

Children

Children

Naotake (adopted)

Children

Yoshihisa

JAPAN
The Showa Era

EMPEROR HIROHITO
The Showa Era

The history of the monarchy of Japan has been varied and often turbulent. Although the present royal family traces its ancestry back to the House of Yamato, which emerged around A.D. 200 as the Imperial rulers, it has only been for a comparatively short period that the monarchy has wielded political power.

The emergence of the samurai class in the eleventh and twelfth centuries saw power being concentrated in the hands of an oligarchy of dominant families. It was at this time (the Kamakura period) that the Shogunate (or military government) first made its appearance. The Shogunate itself was not always able to cope with the decentralising tendencies of the warrior class and the fifteenth and early part of the sixteenth centuries were overshadowed by internecine warfare. Under the rule of the Tokugawa family (Edo Period 1603–1867) Japan underwent a period of prosperity and peace though this was at the expense of isolating the country from world affairs. In the mid-nineteenth century the Tokugawa regime at last broke down and national rule was returned to the Imperial throne. From 1867 onwards Japan, adopting Western institutions and technology, moved rapidly to the forefront among the nation states and now holds a position comparable, despite the disasters of the Second World War, to other major industrial powers.

It is perhaps ironic that, although the Constitution of 1947 excludes the Emperor from power related to government and restricts his role to ceremonial functions (he does appoint the Prime Minister designated by the Diet) his role as a figurehead and symbol is more pronounced than in earlier periods of Japanese history. At a ceremony celebrating the fiftieth anniversary of his accession to the throne the Prime Minister pointed out that the Emperor has stood as a 'significant pillar of the unity of the people'. These are not empty words and are echoed by many Japanese.

His Majesty the Emperor Hirohito was born in Tokyo on 29th April 1901 and studied at the Peer's School and also at a special institute established for his education. Becoming Prince Regent in 1921 he succeeded to the throne on the death of the Emperor Taisho in 1926. By this time he had married the daughter of Prince Kuni; she is the present Empress Nagako. Following the last war the Emperor and Empress have travelled extensively and often around the country, giving aid and support in the attempts to rehabilitate the nation after the ravages of the war. They both take an interest in economic, social and cultural affairs and are often to be seen attending Tree-Planting ceremonies and the National Sports Festival, held annually.

His Majesty is well known as a marine biologist and has had several books on this subject published. Her Majesty is considered an accomplished artist in both Japanese painting and music. They live in the Imperial Palace in the centre of Tokyo on the site of the former Castle of the Tokugawa Shogunate.

Crown Prince Akihito, born on 23rd December 1933, shares his father's interest in marine biology and has had several papers published in the *Japanese Journal of Ichthyology*. He was educated at Gakushuin High School, graduating there in 1952 and subsequently attending the University. He was married in April 1959 to Miss Michiko Shoda and they have two sons and one daughter.

The Emperor and Empress have had six other children; Prince Hitachi, four married daughters – the late Mrs Morihiro Higshikuni (former Princess Teru), Mrs Toshimichi Takasukasa (former Princess Taka), Mrs Takamasa Ikeda (former Princess Yari) and Mrs Hisanegu Shimazu (former Princess Suga) – and one unmarried daughter, Princess Hisa.

His Majesty's years as Emperor are referred to in Japanese as the 'Showa' era. Showa, meaning 'Enlightenment and Peace', was the period name selected by the government at Hirohito's succession.

His Imperial Majesty Emperor Hirohito and his
Empress pose in the grounds of their summer palace
at Nasu.

Opposite During her state visit to Japan in 1975 Queen Elizabeth II called on Crown Prince Akihito and his wife Princess Michiko at Togu Palace, Tokyo, where she met the children of the Crown Prince and Princess.

Right At the Imperial Palace in Tokyo Queen Elizabeth II with the Emperor receive guests for the state banquet.

Bottom right The Emperor entertains Queen Elizabeth II at the Imperial Palace, Tokyo, for the state banquet during the Queen's visit.

Above Crown Prince Akihito with his wife Princess Michiko at the Akasaka Palace, Tokyo.

Opposite Emperor Hirohito with his Empress during their state visit to London in 1971 at Westminster Abbey when they laid a wreath on the tomb of The Unknown Warrior.

Right The Emperor and Empress looking at flower arrangements at their summer palace of Nasu.

Top right The Emperor and
Empress during their state visit to
London in 1971.

Bottom right The Emperor and
Empress with the Crown Prince
and his wife in the gardens at Nasu
Palace.

Below Emperor Hirohito and the
Empress with some of their
favourite birds at Nasu Palace.

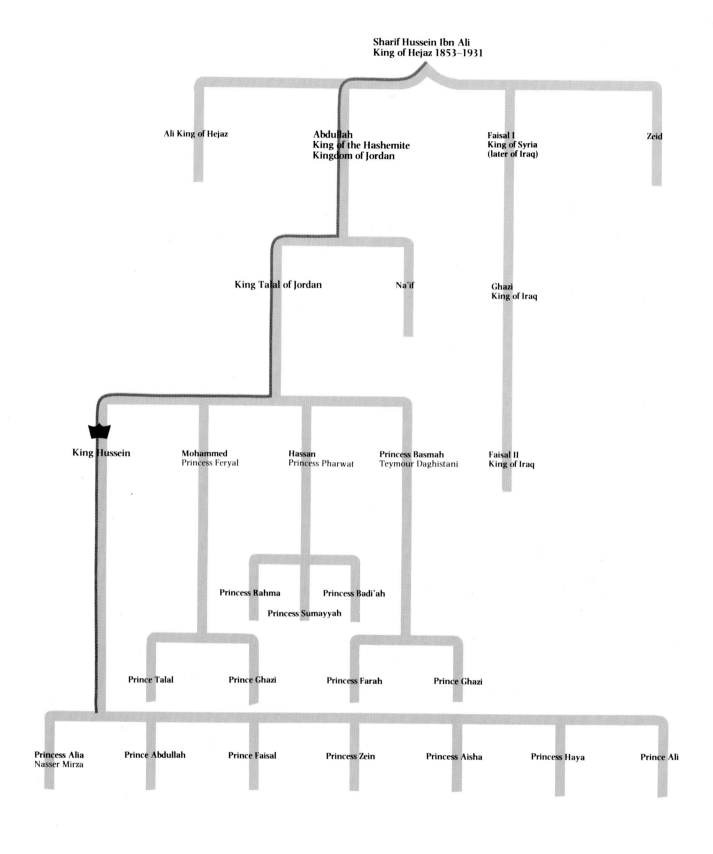

Sharif Hussein Ibn Ali
King of Hejaz 1853–1931

Ali King of Hejaz

Abdullah
King of the Hashemite
Kingdom of Jordan

Faisal I
King of Syria
(later of Iraq)

Zeid

King Talal of Jordan

Na'if

Ghazi
King of Iraq

King Hussein

Mohammed
Princess Feryal

Hassan
Princess Pharwat

Princess Basmah
Teymour Daghistani

Faisal II
King of Iraq

Princess Rahma

Princess Badi'ah

Princess Sumayyah

Prince Talal

Prince Ghazi

Princess Farah

Prince Ghazi

Princess Alia
Nasser Mirza

Prince Abdullah

Prince Faisal

Princess Zein

Princess Aisha

Princess Haya

Prince Ali

JORDAN
The House of Hashem

KING HUSSEIN
Hashemite Kingdom of Jordan

Jordan has had a troubled history. Although a territory where ten millenia ago people first began a settled community life, the land has a record of bloodshed and hardship equal to any other Middle East country.

Four hundred years of Ottoman domination came to an end early in this century when Sharif Hussein (the present king's great-grandfather) proclaimed the Arab Revolt. In 1921 Sharif's second son Abdullah established the Emirate of Trans-Jordan under a British Mandate. This Mandate lasted until 1946 and the Hashemite Kingdom of Jordan became a sovereign state with Emir Abdullah as King.

Abdullah proved to be a wise and benevolent ruler. During his brief reign he established a close rapport with his young grandson Prince Hussein. 'Come always to me and try to learn what you can from what you witness,' the old man said, and Hussein was often to be seen with his grandfather, listening to the problems of his subjects. Perhaps most important of all Hussein acquired a deep religious faith from Abdullah which has since played a major part in his life.

Abdullah's reign was cut short suddenly and tragically by an assassin's bullets in 1951. A year later Hussein became king, aged seventeen. The problems he faced were enormous. Surrounded by hostile states and only recently independent, Jordan was the focus of a great deal of enmity. It was essential that her military capabilities were strengthened and Hussein threw himself into this task with a drive and fervour that have made him one of the foremost Arab military leaders. Soon after he was crowned he learned to fly and made a practice of familiarising himself with every new piece of equipment acquired by the Jordanian forces, from rifles to Sherman tanks. His most difficult military decision was to remove Glubb Pasha, the commander of the Arab Legion. It was a grave risk but ultimately justified; the Jordan-Arab Army under his leadership has played a vital role in establishing the country as a nation state.

But Hussein's greatest achievement has not been as a military leader. He has led his people, by personal example, by courage and by tenacity, to an unprecedented height of prosperity and security. There have been many setbacks: the reoccupation of the West Bank by the Israelis in 1967 and the perennial problem of the Palestinian refugees, not to mention the disruption caused by the presence of Palestinian guerillas, have all posed seemingly insoluble problems. However, the advances are real enough: Jordan now boasts two universities, an industrial and business framework equal to any Arab state, a thriving tourist industry and a medical system unrivalled in the Middle East. All this has been forged from the sands of the desert, the vision of a leader and the resilience of a people. At his Jubilee in 1977 Hussein talked with pride and pleasure about the Jordan that he hoped to create in the next twenty-five years of his reign: 'The Jordanian people have made many sacrifices to build the nation. I want to see the next twenty-five years reward them for these sacrifices.'

The auguries in 1952 were not auspicious. The politicians and the pundits claimed that Hussein would not survive in an area of the world where political dislocation and warfare are endemic. So far he has proved them all wrong. He has had his share of political and personal problems, emerging unscathed from nine assassination attempts and at least one attempted coup. In February 1977 he lost his third wife Queen Alya in an air crash. He still shows the marks of that tragedy but it is to be hoped that he and his young family will find happiness again in his marriage to Elizabeth Halaby, now called Nur Al Hussein.

It is worth recalling an occasion early in Hussein's reign when he rushed to a village that had been attacked by the Israelis, to give comfort and support to the survivors. Passing a tent late at night he heard a Bedouin say: 'Abdullah would be proud of his grandson now.' It is a sentiment that rings as true today as it did then. The partnership of the King and his people has been remarkable and does much to explain their success against heavy odds.

His Majesty King Hussein photographed in the
Persian Gulf.

Above King Hussein escorts Queen Fabiola of Belgium to the Shah and Empress of Iran's private banquet to celebrate 2,500 years of the Persian dynasty at Persepolis, 1971.

Opposite King Hussein with his sister Princess Basmah.

Right A private table, a private talk; King Hussein with Princess Sophie of Spain (now Queen), Queen Anne-Marie and Empress Farah.

Prince Alfred (1842)
Henriette Princess of Liechtenstein

Princess Franziska　　**Prince Franz**　　**Princess**　　**Princess Marie Therise**　　**Prince Johann**
Maria Grafin Andrassy

Prince Heinrich　　**Prince Georg Hartmann**

Prince Alois
Elizabeth Erzherzogin
of Austria

Prince Alfred
Princess Theresia
Ottingen-Ottingen

Prince Karl
Elizabeth Furstin Urach

Wilhelm　　**Maria Joseph**　　**Franziska**　　**Wolfgang**

Maria Benedikte　　**Johann Moritz**　　**Heinrich**　　**Eleonore**

Princess Marie Therise
Arthur Graf Strachwitz

Prince Ulrich　　**Princess Henriette**　　**Prince Alois**　　**Prince Heinrich**
Peter Graf zu Etize

Prince Franz Josef II
Georgine Grafin Wilczek

Prince Karl Alfred
Agnus Erzherzogin
of Austria

Prince Georg
Christine Herzogin
of Worttemberg

Margarita　　**Maria Assunta**　　**Isabelle**　　**Christoph**　　**Marie Helene**　　**Georgine**

Dominik　　**Andreas**　　**Gregor**　　**Alexandra**　　**Maria Pia**

Prince Johann Adam
Marie Aglaë Kinsky

Prince Philipp
Isabel
de L'Arbre d. Malander

Prince Nikolaus　　**Princess Nora**　　**Prince Franz Joseph Wenzel**

Alexander

**Prince
Alois Philippe**　　**Prince
Maximillian**　　**Prince
Constantine**

LIECHTENSTEIN

The House of Liechtenstein

PRINCE FRANZ-JOSEF II
The House of Liechtenstein

The Lords of Liechtenstein first appeared in history in the early half of the twelfth century. It is not known where they originated, but it is thought that they came from the Bavarian Danube area and are descended from the Lords of Donauworth. Hugo was the owner of the castle of Liechtenstein near Modling, south of Vienna, and the family took their name from the castle.

They held important offices in Austria and in 1608, one, Karl, was raised to the rank of Prince. He sided with the House of Hapsburg in the most dangerous period of Austrian history, and during the Thirty Years War became Viceroy in Bohemia and held the highest office at the Imperial court, that of Lord High Steward. From the rich estates in Lower Austria, Mahren and Bohemia, they frequently made loans to the Emperor, and Karl's son was the founder of the collection of paintings which came into being about three hundred years ago, one of the oldest private collections in existence.

Until very recently, Liechtenstein, a tiny principality between the Alps and the Rhine, was unimaginably poor. Composed almost entirely of small struggling farmers, there were no cities, no bourgeoisie, and currency was brought in mainly through travel – by the renting of horses and other forms of transport on the highway to the south. In 1771 there was not a doctor, surgeon or trained midwife in the land.

The people fought constantly against the forces of nature: the Rhine hurtling through the gorges making a swampy wilderness of the valley, and the sudden storms sweeping down the mountains bringing torrents of water and gravel in their wake. Only in the last century was it possible to contain the Rhine and in this century to control the massive gravel slides.

Prince Johann I (1805-36) was the first of the country's rulers to concern himself with his people's welfare, introducing compulsory education – there were no schools – the Austrian Civil and Criminal Code, and the registering of Landed Property. Serfdom was abolished. The country had been occupied for the last time in 1799 after the Wars of Coalition against the armies of the French Revolution. Sovereignty was established in 1806 and has never been lost again.

With Johann II in the mid-nineteenth century came further reforms. Known as Johann the Good, he concluded a customs treaty with Switzerland and was a great friend and benefactor of the arts. Franz I who succeeded him in 1929, was the first ruling Prince to be frequently in the country for any period of time, and Franz-Josef II, the present ruler, is the first to take up actual residence in the principality.

Born in 1906 at Castle Fauenthal in Steiermark, Austria, the first son of Prince Alois and H.R.H. the Archduchess Elisabeth Amalie of Austria, the Emperor of Austria was his godfather. Some three years of his childhood were spent at the Castle Gross-Ullersdorf, important years since it was then that he discovered his great love of nature which decided his future profession.

Favourite subjects at school were Mathematics, Greek, and Natural History, which determined his following forestry studies at the Agricultural High School in Vienna. Hunting, skiing and swimming in his spare time, he passed his examinations in the Diploma for Forestry Engineering in 1929, travelled extensively throughout Europe and overseas, and in March 1938, was appointed Regent by Prince Franz I. In July of the same year, the Prince died. Franz-Josef succeeded him and the people of Liechtenstein took their Oath of Allegiance on 29th May 1939. In August 1976 his immense popularity was demonstrated when the Principality celebrated his seventieth birthday.

In 1943, the Prince married Countess Georgine von Wilczek. Born in Graz, Austria, in 1921, she went first to convent school in Vienna and then to Rome. Returning to Vienna, she studied cultural arts and crafts and finally became a successful dress designer. She had inherited her mother's talent for languages and passed her interpreter's examination in English, French and Italian. The Princess takes an active part in many charitable organizations and during the Hungarian Revolution in 1956, helped in a refugee camp. The Prince and Princess have close connections with the British Royal Family. They attended Princess Anne's wedding in 1973 and are frequent visitors at the Windsor Horse Show, sharing Prince Philip's interest in driving four-in-hand.

Five children have been born of the marriage: Prince Johann Adam in 1945; Prince Philipp in 1946; Prince Nikolaus in 1947; Princess Nora in 1950 and Prince Franz Joseph Wenzel in 1962. There are several grandchildren.

Prince Franz-Josef II and his wife Princess Georgina.

Above Princess Georgina with
Prince Franz-Josef II, when they
attended the celebrations in Iran of
the 2,500 years of the Persian
dynasty.

Right Prince Franz-Josef II and
Princess Georgina in their home in
Vaduz Castle with their dog
'Vodka'.

Left Crown Prince Adam with his wife Princess Marie.

Opposite Prince Franz-Josef II with his son Prince Adam and his wife in the grounds of their home at Castle Vaduz.

Below Princess Georgina in the grounds of Vaduz Castle.

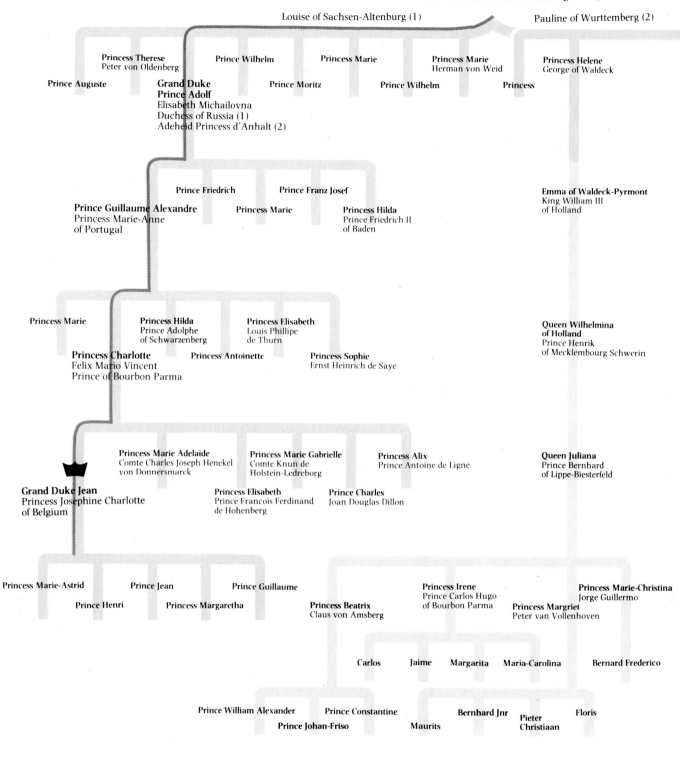

Prince Wilhelm of Nassau Weilburg

Louise of Sachsen-Altenburg (1)   Pauline of Wurttemberg (2)

Princess Therese
Peter von Oldenberg

Prince Wilhelm

Princess Marie

Princess Marie
Herman von Weid

Princess Helene
George of Waldeck

Prince Auguste

**Grand Duke
Prince Adolf**
Elisabeth Michailovna
Duchess of Russia (1)
Adeheid Princess d'Anhalt (2)

Prince Moritz

Prince Wilhelm

Princess

Prince Friedrich

Prince Franz Josef

Emma of Waldeck-Pyrmont
King William III
of Holland

Prince Guillaume Alexandre
Princess Marie-Anne
of Portugal

Princess Marie

Princess Hilda
Prince Friedrich II
of Baden

Princess Marie

Princess Hilda
Prince Adolphe
of Schwarzenberg

Princess Elisabeth
Louis Phillipe
de Thurn

**Queen Wilhelmina
of Holland**
Prince Henrik
of Mecklembourg Schwerin

Princess Charlotte
Felix Mario Vincent
Prince of Bourbon Parma

Princess Antoinette

Princess Sophie
Ernst Heinrich de Saye

Princess Marie Adelaide
Comte Charles Joseph Henekel
von Donnersmarck

Princess Marie Gabrielle
Comte Knun de
Holstein-Ledreborg

Princess Alix
Prince Antoine de Ligne

Queen Juliana
Prince Bernhard
of Lippe-Biesterfeld

Grand Duke Jean
Princess Josephine Charlotte
of Belgium

Princess Elisabeth
Prince Francois Ferdinand
de Hohenberg

Prince Charles
Joan Douglas Dillon

Princess Marie-Astrid

Prince Jean

Prince Guillaume

Princess Irene
Prince Carlos Hugo
of Bourbon Parma

Princess Marie-Christina
Jorge Guillermo

Prince Henri

Princess Margaretha

Princess Beatrix
Claus von Amsberg

Princess Margriet
Peter van Vollenhoven

Carlos   Jaime   Margarita   Maria-Carolina   Bernard Frederico

Prince William Alexander   Prince Constantine   **Bernhard Jnr**   **Pieter Christiaan**   **Floris**

Prince Johan-Friso   Maurits

Princess Sophie
King Oscar II
of Sweden

nce Nicolaus
talie von Pushkine

King Gustaf V
of Sweden
Victoria Princess
of Baden

King Gustaf VI Adolf
Princess Margaret
of Great Britain (1)
Princess Louise Mountbatten

Princess Ingrid
King Frederik IX
of Denmark

LUXEMBOURG
The House of Nassau

Queen Margrethe II   **Princess Benedikte**   **Princess Anne Marie**
Henry de Monpezat   Prince Richard   King Constantine
                          of Sayn-Wittgenstein   of Greece
                          Berleburg

          Gustav   **Alexandra**   **Nathalie**

e Frederik   **Prince Joachim**   **Princess Alexia**   **Prince Paul**   **Prince Nicolaos**

GRAND DUKE JEAN
The House of Nassau

At the Congress of Vienna in 1815, it was decided that the Grand Duchy of Luxembourg should be given to the King of the Netherlands, William 1st Prince of Orange-Nassau, to be owned perpetually and personally by him and his legitimate successors. Until 1890 this decision remained unaltered, but when William III died leaving no male descendant, the Grand Duke Adolphe became founder of the Luxembourg dynasty.

The present Grand Duke Jean (Benoit – Guillaume – Robert – Antoine – Louis – Marie – Adolphe – Marc d'Aviano), Duke of Nassau, Prince of Bourbon, Prince of Parma, is the fifth sovereign of the Grand Duchy. Born in Luxembourg on 5th January 1921, he is the eldest son of the Grand Duchess Charlotte, daughter of the Infanta of Portugal, and Prince Felix, Prince of Bourbon Parma and direct descendant of the kings of France. His Holiness Pope Benedict XV was his godfather.

Much of his childhood was spent at the family home, the Chateau de Colmar-Berg, but when he was thirteen he came to England to continue his education at Ampleforth College in Yorkshire. As Hereditary Prince, he came of age when he was eighteen and in 1939 assumed the titles of Hereditary Grand Duke of Luxembourg, Hereditary Prince of Nassau and Prince of Bourbon Parma.

The following year, German troops invaded the Grand Duchy and the entire family and government left for France and a Chateau outside Paris placed at their disposal by the French government. From here, they made their way south through Spain to Portugal. The Grand Duchess went on to London which became the official seat of her government. The children with their father travelled to America in a warship sent by President Roosevelt, and finally arrived in Canada. The family settled down surprisingly quickly. The Hereditary Grand Duke Jean made an impressive series of broadcasts appealing for support for the over-run countries of Europe, and was admitted to the University of Quebec to read Law and Political Science.

In 1942, he left with his father Prince Felix, to volunteer for service with the British army. Initially attached to the Northern Command, the Prince was with the first allied troops to relieve the con-centration camp at Dachau. His son joined the Irish Guards, and five days after the Normandy landings in June 1944, was at Bayeux with his battalion. They entered Brussels on 3rd September and within a week had crossed the Luxembourg frontier at the exact place at which the family had crossed in the opposite direction when they fled into exile. Prince Jean and his escort group arrived in the city of Luxembourg a few hours after his father had reached there with the American 5th Armoured Division on 10th September 1944. He rejoined his unit but was back to take part in the triumphal return from exile of his mother, the Grand Duchess, on 14th April 1945.

In May, the Prince was seconded from his regiment to serve as Liaison Officer to the Allied Military Mission in Luxembourg. Later that year he was nominated Colonel of the newly formed Luxembourg army and finally became Assistant Inspector-General.

From 1951 to 1961, he was a member of the State Council and was closely concerned with the legal and political life of his country. Then in 1953 he married Her Royal Highness Princess Josephine Charlotte of Belgium, sister of King Baudouin, at the Cathedral of our Lady in Luxembourg. From that moment, Josephine Charlotte became Hereditary Grand Duchess – until her husband's accession, when she took the title of Grand Duchess. They have five children: Princess Marie-Astrid born 17th February 1954; Prince Henri 16th April 1955; Prince Jean and Princess Margretha 15th May 1957; and Prince Guillaume 1st May 1963.

In 1961, the Grand Duchess Charlotte appointed her son Jean Lieutenant-Representative, a most solemn appointment since all acts from then on performed by him in execution of this mandate had the same effect as if performed by herself.

Less than four years later, on 12th November 1964, after a reign of forty-five years, she signed the declaration of abdication and Prince Jean achieved the full status of Grand Duke.

As the European Community has grown so has the role played by Luxembourg in international affairs, and the Grand Duke has taken an increasingly active part in the organisation of the Community.

Their Royal Highnesses Grand Duke Jean
and Grand Duchess Josephine Charlotte.

Above A very informal family
gathering in the lounge of the
Grand Ducal Palace, as Princess
Josephine Charlotte plays the
piano.

Opposite The Luxembourg Royal
Family photographed in the Blue
Lounge of the Grand Ducal Palace.

Right Grand Duke Jean with
Princess Marie-Astrid and Princess
Margaretha.

Grand Duke Jean.

Left Crown Prince Henri with his sister Princess Marie-Astrid.

Above A charming yet formal Princess Marie-Astrid.

Above Princess Marie-Astrid with 'Cyrus' in the grounds of her home.

Right The Luxembourg Royal Family – Prince Guillaume, Princess Margaretha, Prince Jean, the Grand Duke and Duchess, Princess Marie-Astrid and Crown Prince Henri with their family dog 'Cyrus', in the grounds of their home, Colmar Berg Castle.

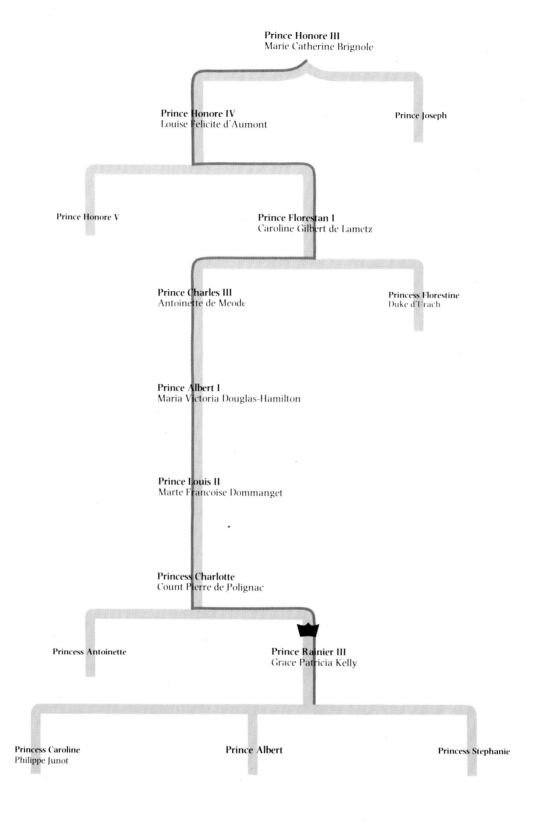

Prince Honore III
Marie Catherine Brignole

Prince Honore IV
Louise Felicite d'Aumont

Prince Joseph

Prince Honore V

Prince Florestan I
Caroline Gilbert de Lametz

Prince Charles III
Antoinette de Meode

Princess Florestine
Duke d'Urach

Prince Albert I
Maria Victoria Douglas-Hamilton

Prince Louis II
Marte Francoise Dommanget

Princess Charlotte
Count Pierre de Polignac

Princess Antoinette

Prince Rainier III
Grace Patricia Kelly

Princess Caroline
Philippe Junot

Prince Albert

Princess Stephanie

MONACO
The House of Grimaldi

PRINCE RAINIER III
The House of Grimaldi

Since primitive times, the fine geographical position of the Rock of Monaco has attracted many races. The Phoenicians, Romans, Barbarians, all attempted to take and keep it. In 1197, the Genoese acquired possession of the territory but until 1419 there was a continuous change of ownership between Ghibellines who were partisans of the Emperor Frederick I of Barberossa, and Guelfs, faithful to the Pope, of which the Grimaldi family were a part. Rainier I of Monaco who was a Grimaldi and Jean I, son of Rainier II, finally established the family authority over the country.

In 1499, Louis XII of France declared himself responsible for the protection of their fortress, and sixteen years later recognised Monaco's independence. But there was no easy path to peace and progress, with an assassination, Spanish 'Protection', imprisonment and unification with the French Republic all clouding the dream of total independence. In 1612, Honore II took the title of Prince and Lord of Monaco, setting the style for future rulers. In 1814 independence did become reality for three brief years, but was followed by a further spell of 'protection', this time from Sardinia. Not until 1861 was Monaco's independence finally established, when it became one of the smallest states in the world.

Albert I, scientist and idealist, succeeded to the throne in 1889. Believing passionately in concord between peoples, he founded amongst other institutions, one to promote international peace, another for the study of oceanography. He also created the automobile rally. His son Louis II succeeded him in 1922. Two years earlier, Louis' daughter Charlotte had married Count Pierre de Polignac who took the name and arms of Grimaldi, substituting them for his own. A daughter, Antoinette, was born of the marriage, then a son, Rainier, in whose favour his mother resigned her rights to the Throne.

With the Second World War, a state of war was necessarily imposed on the country on account of its geographical position. Louis became a general in the French army, his heir and grandson Rainier, a sub-lieutenant. In 1945, following a series of Franco-Monegasque Conventions, the citizens of Monaco returned once more to their normal way of life. Four years later, Louis II died and his grandson became Prince of Monaco.

Few rulers could have wider ranging interests than Rainier III. He founded the International Television Festival, the Literary Council of the principality, the International Centre for Human Problems and the Scientific Centre. In memory of his father, he created the Prince Pierre of Monaco Foundation to encourage culture and the arts; he instituted Palace concerts and a Prix de Composition Musicale, and in 1956 married the lovely Grace Kelly.

Their palace is high on a hill overlooking the harbour of Monte Carlo with its busy traffic of yachts, long hours of sunshine and wealth of flowers. They have three children: Caroline Louise Marguerite born in 1957; Albert Alexandre Louis Pierre, the Hereditary Prince, born in 1958; and Stephanie Marie Elisabeth born in 1965. Princess Caroline has received a fair share of the family publicity. This has been due as much to her beauty as to her apparent penchant for the night life of Paris. She was married in the summer of 1978 to M. Philippe Junot, a French businessman.

Among the many activities of Princess Grace, she has opened a boutique, 'La Boutique du Rocher', to give local craftsmen and artists an opportunity of showing their work at minimum cost. Handwoven and knitted goods, olive wood carving, ceramics, dried flowers and a great variety of exclusively hand made pieces are on regular exhibition.

It is a fascinating commentary on the changes wrought in Monaco that its early history was dominated by an urgent desire to keep people out. Today, the Prince pursues a steady policy of building and development in order to bring visitors into the country, and make Monaco a first class modern tourist centre.

Their Serene Highnesses Prince Rainier and his wife
Princess Grace.

Above The Royal Family of Monaco.

Opposite above Prince Rainier with his wife, Princess Grace and their children, Prince Albert and Princess Caroline, when they attended a party to celebrate 25 years of his reign, 1974.

Right The engagement of Princess Caroline of Monaco to Mr Philippe Junot – a family group in the gardens of the Monaco Royal Palace, 1977.

Far right The Royal Family of Monaco at the celebration day party, in full national costume, in 1974.

Above Princess Caroline of Monaco enjoying an evening out with her fiancé Mr Philippe Junot.

Right Their Serene Highnesses with Princess Anne, 1972, in the Royal box of the Opera House, Monte Carlo.

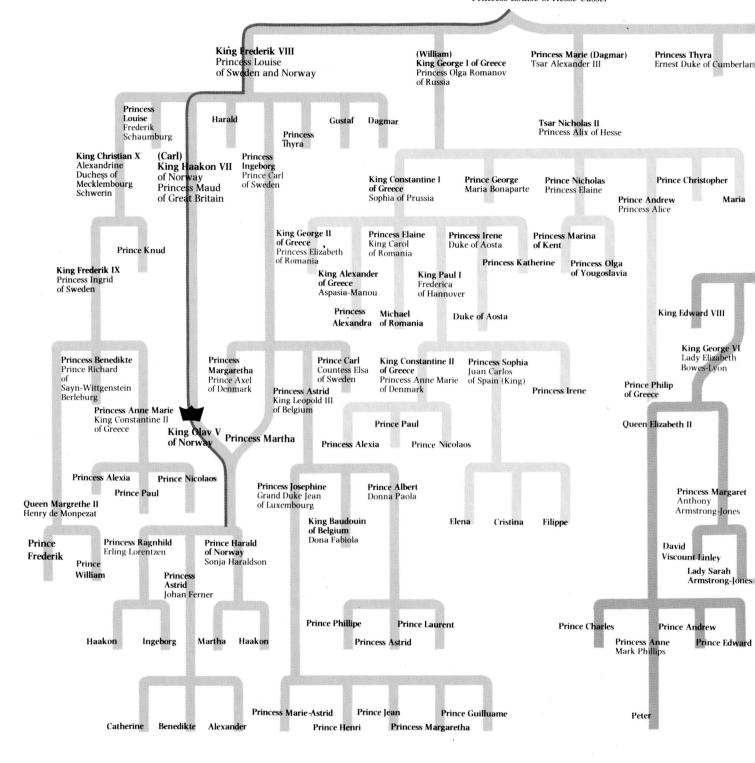

**King Christian IX
of Denmark**
Princess Louise of Hesse-Cassel

King Frederik VIII
Princess Louise
of Sweden and Norway

**(William)
King George I of Greece**
Princess Olga Romanov
of Russia

Princess Marie (Dagmar)
Tsar Alexander III

Princess Thyra
Ernest Duke of Cumberland

**Princess
Louise**
Frederik
Schaumburg

Harald

Gustaf **Dagmar**

**Princess
Thyra**

Tsar Nicholas II
Princess Alix of Hesse

King Christian X
Alexandrine
Duchess of
Mecklembourg
Schwerin

**(Carl)
King Haakon VII
of Norway**
Princess Maud
of Great Britain

**Princess
Ingeborg**
Prince Carl
of Sweden

**King Constantine I
of Greece**
Sophia of Prussia

Prince George
Maria Bonaparte

Prince Nicholas
Princess Elaine

Prince Christopher

Prince Andrew
Princess Alice

Maria

Prince Knud

**King George II
of Greece**
Princess Elizabeth
of Romania

Princess Elaine
King Carol
of Romania

Princess Irene
Duke of Aosta

**Princess Marina
of Kent**

King Frederik IX
Princess Ingrid
of Sweden

Princess Katherine

**Princess Olga
of Yougoslavia**

**King Alexander
of Greece**
Aspasia-Manou

King Paul I
Frederica
of Hannover

**Princess
Alexandra**

**Michael
of Romania**

Duke of Aosta

King Edward VIII

King George VI
Lady Elizabeth
Bowes-Lyon

Princess Benedikte
Prince Richard
of
Sayn-Wittgenstein
Berleburg

**Princess
Margaretha**
Prince Axel
of Denmark

Prince Carl
Countess Elsa
of Sweden

**King Constantine II
of Greece**
Princess Anne Marie
of Denmark

Princess Sophia
Juan Carlos
of Spain (King)

**Prince Philip
of Greece**

Princess Astrid
King Leopold III
of Belgium

Princess Irene

Princess Anne Marie
King Constantine II
of Greece

Prince Paul

Queen Elizabeth II

**King Olav V
of Norway** **Princess Martha**

Princess Alexia **Prince Nicolaos**

Princess Alexia
Prince Paul

Prince Nicolaos

Princess Josephine
Grand Duke Jean
of Luxembourg

Prince Albert
Donna Paola

Princess Margaret
Anthony
Armstrong-Jones

Queen Margrethe II
Henry de Monpezat

**King Baudouin
of Belgium**
Dona Fabiola

Elena **Cristina** **Filippe**

**David
Viscount Linley**

**Prince
Frederik**

Princess Ragnhild
Erling Lorentzen

**Prince Harald
of Norway**
Sonja Haraldson

**Lady Sarah
Armstrong-Jones**

**Prince
William**

**Princess
Astrid**
Johan Ferner

Prince Phillipe **Prince Laurent**

Princess Astrid

Prince Charles **Prince Andrew**

Princess Anne
Mark Phillips

Prince Edward

Haakon **Ingeborg** **Martha** **Haakon**

Princess Marie-Astrid **Prince Jean** **Prince Guilluame**

Prince Henri **Princess Margaretha**

Peter

Catherine **Benedikte** **Alexander**

Prince Waldemar
Marie Dr. of
Duc. de Chartres

Princess Alexandra
King Edward VIII
of Great Britain

Prince Aage

Prince Albert

Princess Louise
Duke of Fife

Princess Maud
King Haakon VII
of Norway

King George V
Princess Mary
of Teck

Princess Victoria

Prince Alexander

Alexandra   Maud

King Olav V
of Norway

Princess Royal
(Mary)
Viscount Lascelles

Prince Henry
Duke of Gloucester
Lady Alice Scott

Prince John

See family of
King Frederik VIII

Hon. Gerald David
Lascelles

Prince George
Duke of Kent
Princess Marina
of Greece

George Henry Huber
Earl of Harewood

Prince
William

Prince Richard

Duke of Kent
Katherine Worsley

Princess Alexandra
Hon Angus Ogilvy

Prince Michael

George
Earl of St. Andrews

Lady Helen
Windsor

James   Marina

NORWAY
The House of Glücksborg

KING OLAV V
The House of Glücksborg

Norway, like so many other Teutonic countries, once consisted of small districts, each headed by a king chosen by the people. Towards the end of the ninth century, one of the kings, Harald the Fairheaded, swore that he would not cut his hair or beard until he had collected the whole of Norway under one crown. Around 900, the great sea battle of Hafrsfjord was fought when Harald finally overcame his rivals, and this is considered the beginning of the Kingdom of Norway. Olav the Saint, proclaimed king in 1015, introduced christianity to the country, and the first recorded coronation was of Magnus V Erlingson in Bergen in 1163.

In 1319, the three-year-old Magnus Ericsson succeeded to the throne as king of a short-lived union of Norway and Sweden. In 1387, when the boy king Olav died, the royal line became extinct, and the crown passed to his mother, Margrete, daughter of the King of Denmark. This marked the beginning of union with Denmark which was to last four centuries. Christopher of Bavaria was crowned King of Norway, Denmark and Sweden in 1442 and eight years later, Christian of Oldenburg, claimant to the Danish throne, was proclaimed King of Norway, eliminating Karl VIII of Sweden and ending the union of the three kingdoms.

After the reformation, Norway became little more than a province of Denmark. By the Treaty of Kiel in 1814, Frederick VI was forced to cede Norway to Sweden, and not until 1905 did the country break away from monarchy to the union and choose the Danish Prince Carl, grandson of Christian IX of Denmark, as King. Two years earlier, Carl had been staying with his wife Princess Maud, daughter of Edward VII of Britain, at Appleton House in Sandringham, Norfolk, and it was here that on 2nd July 1903, Olav V of Norway was born.

After the dissolution of the union with Sweden, Carl changed his own name to Haakon and that of his baby son Alexander, to Olav. Schooling for the boy was democratic to a degree. Apart from early years with a tutor at the Palace, he went to school in Oslo and at the request of his parents received no special privileges. He graduated from the Military Academy, took the oath of allegiance to the Constitution, and in 1924 went to Balliol College, Oxford, where he made many friends and read history and political economy for two years. He was a fine sportsman, a first class skier and has enjoyed a world wide reputation as a yachtsman – he represented Norway in the Olympic Games of 1928 and won the Gold Medal in the six-metre class with a completely amateur crew.

In 1929 he married Princess Martha of Sweden. They had three children: Ragnhild born in 1930, Astrid in 1932 and Harald in 1937 – the first prince to be born in Norway for approximately six hundred years. Olav attained the rank of General of the Army and Admiral of the Navy and in 1939, visited the United States with Princess Martha. They went primarily to see the old Norwegian settlements in the Middle West, but formed a lasting friendship with President Roosevelt that was to prove invaluable in the years that followed.

Germany attacked and occupied Norway in 1940. The King and Olav came to Britain while the Crown Princess and the children were received as guests of the President of the United States, staying there for the rest of the war. Olav divided his time between America and Britain, organising the armed forces of his country abroad, and in 1944 was appointed Commander-in-Chief, returning to Norway one week after the German capitulation.

In 1954 he suffered the tragic loss of his wife. Three years later, on the 21st September 1957, his father died, and the Crown Prince became Olav V of Norway. He has suffered for some years from ill health but continues to undertake his duties as Head of State with resolution and panache. Many of his responsibilities are shared with his son Crown Prince Harald and daughter-in-law Princess Sonja. The couple have two children; Martha Louise and Haakon.

His Majesty King Olav V.

Right Crown Prince Harald.

Opposite Crown Prince Harald and
Crown Princess Sonja in
Stockholm when they attended
the wedding of King Carl Gustaf
of Sweden to Miss Silvia
Sommerlath in 1976.

Below King Olav joins Queen
Ingrid of Denmark and King
Baudouin of Belgium (centre)
with his sister Grand Duchess
Josephine Charlotte of Luxem-
bourg at the celebrations in
Persepolis, Iran, in 1971.

Above Crown Prince Harald with his wife Crown Princess Sonja escort Princess Anne to Tonsberg to attend an open-air concert, during Princess Anne's visit to Norway in 1971.

Opposite above King Olav in relaxed dress in Oslo prior to sailing in the harbour.

Right Crown Prince Harald with his wife Crown Princess Sonja attending the wedding of Princess Christina of Sweden to Mr Tord Magnusen in the Chapel Royal in Stockholm in June, 1974. On their right is Princess Désire of Sweden with her husband Baron Niclas Silfverschiold and on the right of picture is Princess Benedikte of Denmark with her husband Prince Richard of Berleburg. June 1974.

Left Crown Princess Sonja in formal pose.

Opposite Crown Princess Sonja with her children

Below Crown Prince Harald with his wife and their children Martha and Haakon.

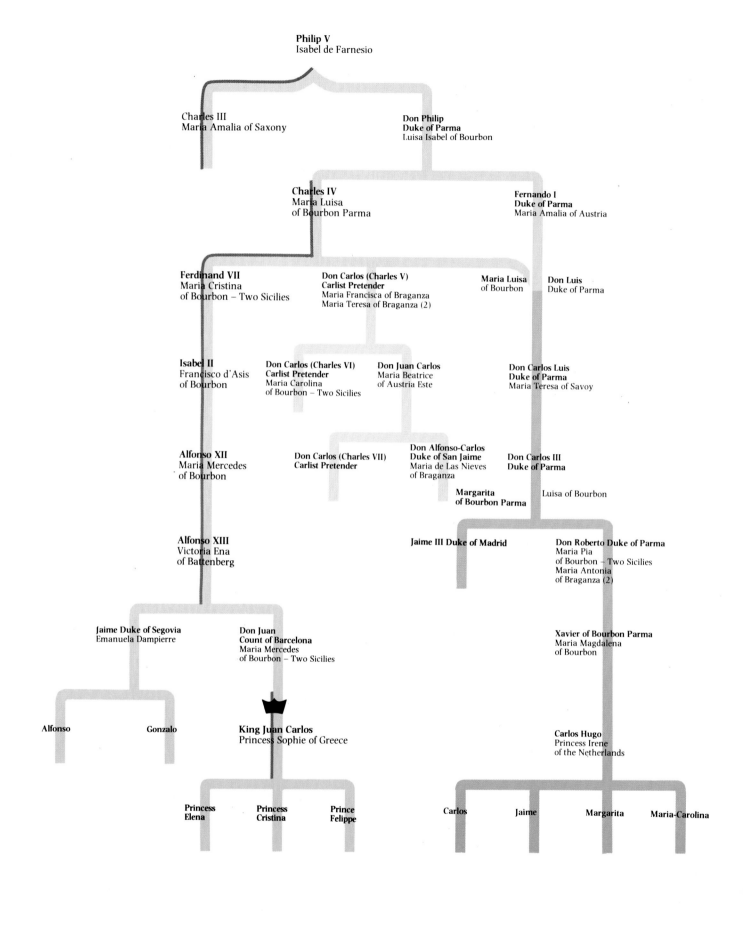

Philip V
Isabel de Farnesio

Charles III
Maria Amalia of Saxony

Don Philip
Duke of Parma
Luisa Isabel of Bourbon

Charles IV
Maria Luisa
of Bourbon Parma

Fernando I
Duke of Parma
Maria Amalia of Austria

Ferdinand VII
Maria Cristina
of Bourbon – Two Sicilies

Don Carlos (Charles V)
Carlist Pretender
Maria Francisca of Braganza
Maria Teresa of Braganza (2)

Maria Luisa
of Bourbon

Don Luis
Duke of Parma

Isabel II
Francisco d'Asis
of Bourbon

Don Carlos (Charles VI)
Carlist Pretender
Maria Carolina
of Bourbon – Two Sicilies

Don Juan Carlos
Maria Beatrice
of Austria Este

Don Carlos Luis
Duke of Parma
Maria Teresa of Savoy

Alfonso XII
Maria Mercedes
of Bourbon

Don Carlos (Charles VII)
Carlist Pretender

Don Alfonso-Carlos
Duke of San Jaime
Maria de Las Nieves
of Braganza

Don Carlos III
Duke of Parma

Margarita
of Bourbon Parma

Luisa of Bourbon

Alfonso XIII
Victoria Ena
of Battenberg

Jaime III Duke of Madrid

Don Roberto Duke of Parma
Maria Pia
of Bourbon – Two Sicilies
Maria Antonia
of Braganza (2)

Jaime Duke of Segovia
Emanuela Dampierre

Don Juan
Count of Barcelona
Maria Mercedes
of Bourbon – Two Sicilies

Xavier of Bourbon Parma
Maria Magdalena
of Bourbon

Alfonso

Gonzalo

King Juan Carlos
Princess Sophie of Greece

Carlos Hugo
Princess Irene
of the Netherlands

Princess
Elena

Princess
Cristina

Prince
Felippe

Carlos

Jaime

Margarita

Maria-Carolina

SPAIN
The House of Bourbon

JUAN CARLOS I
The House of Bourbon

General Franco's death on 20th November 1975 heralded the emergence of Spain's first king for forty-four years. During that time the country had seen first a Republican government and then Franco's regime. The new king, Juan Carlos, is the grandson of the last monarch, King Alfonso XIII. He assumed power under the terms of the Constitution at the onset of Franco's last illness in 1975 at which point he took on all the functions of Head of State.

Although Juan Carlos had been the likely successor to Franco since 1947 there had always been the possibility of severe political dislocation at the occasion of the transfer of power. As it happened Juan Carlos assumed control with the minimum of upheaval. This was perhaps mainly due to the respect in which Juan Carlos was held, particularly by the military, and this can be directly attributed to the educational programme designed for the Prince from an early age.

Juan Carlos is the elder and only surviving son of Don Juan, the Count of Barcelona, who had been designated claimant by his father King Alfonso. He was born in Rome on 5th January 1938 and began his education in Lausanne. Following Franco's decision in 1947 to declare Spain to be a kingdom his education was geared to the possibility of his eventual succession. He entered the Instituto San Isidro Madrid, from 1954 having a personal tutor and a largely military education. He attended the Navy Orphans' College and the Academia General Militar at Zaragoza, being commissioned as a Lieutenant in the army in 1957. He also trained at the Naval Academy, Marin and the Aviation Academy, St Xavier, becoming an Air Force officer in 1960.

As a result of meetings between Don Juan and Franco in 1960 the young Prince undertook a two-year programme at the University of Madrid where he studied the history of Spain, Spanish literature, law, philosophy and economics. From 1963 to 1968 he was attached to various Ministries. Affirmation of his status as Franco's heir came in 1969 when the General announced Juan Carlos as his successor and the Prince took his oath as future King of Spain, swearing loyalty to the principles of the National Movement.

Juan Carlos was married on 14th May 1962 to Princess Sophie, elder daughter of King Paul of the Hellenes and a sister of the former King Constantine. Queen Sofia, as she is now known, speaks several languages and has taken various courses at the University of Madrid. The couple have three children; Dona Elena, born in 1963, Dona Cristina born in 1965 and Don Felippe, the heir, born in 1968. For his christening his great-grandmother, Queen Victoria Eugenie, returned to Spain for the first time since 1931 and was greeted by enthusiastic crowds.

There can be little doubt that as a figurehead Juan Carlos is an admirable choice. He is personable, a hard worker and his interests have great popular appeal. He is an excellent sailor and enjoys flying and racing motor-cars. However, he is more than just a figurehead, being invested with many powers, with the constitutional authority to select and dismiss Prime Ministers as well as having authority over the armed forces with which he enjoys a close rapport largely due to his long military career. Having overcome the initial hurdle of shouldering Franco's responsibilities, and having indicated his desire to pursue more liberal policies than his predecessor, Spain may look forward to a progressive and enlightened regime under Juan Carlos' guidance.

King Juan Carlos I and Queen Sophie.

124

Right Her Majesty Queen Sophie
(as Princess Sophie) when she
attended the Iranian Celebrations
for the 25th centenary of the
Persian dynasty at Persepolis. In
the background can be seen
Marshal Tito of Yugoslavia.

Above Queen Sophie in one of the
lounges at Zarzuela Palace, with
her children, Princesses Elena and
Cristina and Crown Prince
Felippe.

Opposite The Spanish royal family
pose with their dog 'Mika'.

Right King Juan Carlos I and
Queen Sophie in the grounds of
their home at Zarzuela Palace,
Madrid.

Above King Juan Carlos and Queen Sophie enjoy the fun of a motor bike ride in the grounds of Zarzuela Palace.

Opposite The Spanish royal children in the grounds of their home.

Above King Juan Carlos at the controls of his helicopter.

Opposite King Juan Carlos (as Prince) with his cheetah 'Sulki', a gift from Ethiopia.

Right Queen Sophie with two miniature ponies (a gift from the Argentine) in a drawing-room of her home.

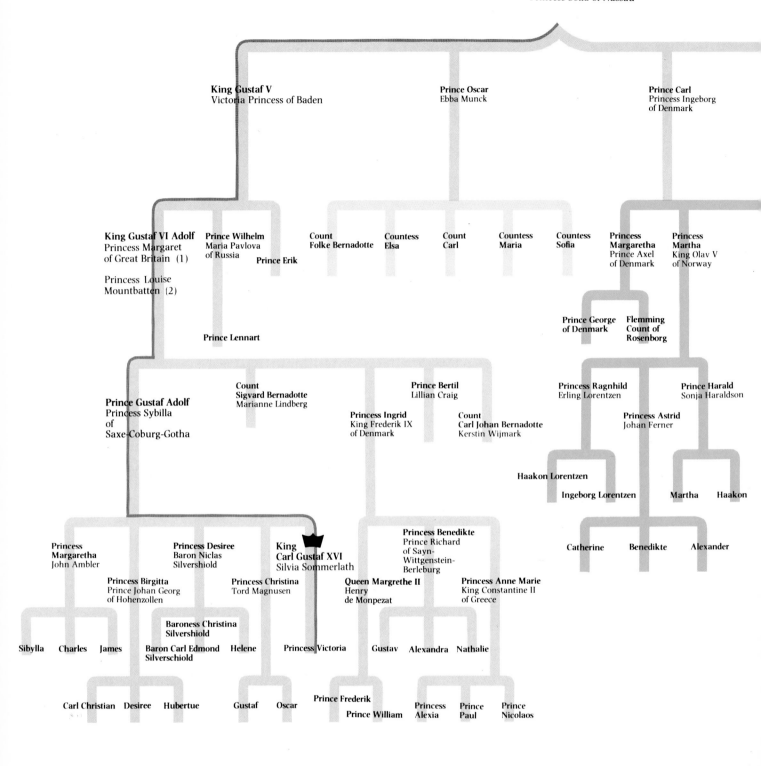

King Oscar II
Princess Sofia of Nassau

King Gustaf V
Victoria Princess of Baden

Prince Oscar
Ebba Munck

Prince Carl
Princess Ingeborg
of Denmark

King Gustaf VI Adolf
Princess Margaret
of Great Britain (1)

Princess Louise
Mountbatten (2)

Prince Wilhelm
Maria Pavlova
of Russia

Prince Erik

Count
Folke Bernadotte

Countess
Elsa

Count
Carl

Countess
Maria

Countess
Sofia

Princess
Margaretha
Prince Axel
of Denmark

Princess
Martha
King Olav V
of Norway

Prince George
of Denmark

Flemming
Count of
Rosenborg

Prince Lennart

Prince Gustaf Adolf
Princess Sybilla
of
Saxe-Coburg-Gotha

Count
Sigvard Bernadotte
Marianne Lindberg

Prince Bertil
Lillian Craig

Princess Ingrid
King Frederik IX
of Denmark

Count
Carl Johan Bernadotte
Kerstin Wijmark

Princess Ragnhild
Erling Lorentzen

Prince Harald
Sonja Haraldson

Princess Astrid
Johan Ferner

Haakon Lorentzen

Ingeborg Lorentzen

Martha

Haakon

Princess
Margaretha
John Ambler

Princess Desiree
Baron Niclas
Silvershiold

King
Carl Gustaf XVI
Silvia Sommerlath

Princess Benedikte
Prince Richard
of Sayn-
Wittgenstein-
Berleburg

Catherine

Benedikte

Alexander

Princess Birgitta
Prince Johan Georg
of Hohenzollen

Princess Christina
Tord Magnusen

Queen Margrethe II
Henry
de Monpezat

Princess Anne Marie
King Constantine II
of Greece

Baroness Christina
Silvershiold

Sibylla

Charles

James

Baron Carl Edmond
Silverschiold

Helene

Princess Victoria

Gustav

Alexandra

Nathalie

Carl Christian

Desiree

Hubertue

Gustaf

Oscar

Prince Frederik

Prince William

Princess
Alexia

Prince
Paul

Prince
Nicolaos

Prince Eugen

Princess Astrid
King Leopold III
of Belgium

Prince Carl
Countess Elsa
of Sweden

Madeleine

King Baudouin
of Belgium
Dona Fabiola
of Spain

Princess Josephine
Grand Duke Jean
of Luxembourg

Prince Albert
Donna Paola
of Italy

Princess Astrid

Prince Philippe

Prince Laurent

Princess
Marie-Astrid

Prince
Henri

Prince
Jean

Princess
Margaretha

Prince
Guillaume

SWEDEN
The House of Bernadotte

KING CARL XVI GUSTAF

The House of Bernadotte

Since the accession of King Carl Gustaf, Sweden has seen many changes in the position of the monarchy. The Constitution of 1975 has radically altered the King's status. He can no longer appoint or discharge Ministers, nor can he participate in government meetings or sign Bills. His duties are now mainly ceremonial and his political influence is much less pronounced than that of his grandfather the late King Gustaf VI. Nevertheless he is still the Head of State and the 'unifying representative and symbol for the entire realm'.

Carl Gustaf is among the youngest of European sovereigns. He was born on 30th April 1946, suffering the loss of his father in an air crash when he was less than a year old. His mother was a niece of Princess Alice of Athlone and his paternal grandmother was Princess Margaret of Connaught. Thus like many other members of European royal families he is descended from Queen Victoria.

The King received a general education; he attended a co-educational boarding school at Sigtuna near Stockholm, passing the university entrance examination in 1966. This was followed by two years military service where he served in a torpedo-boat unit, taking the Naval Staff examinations in 1969. He then spent a year at the University of Uppsala.

The King's grandfather and predecessor Gustaf VI took a special interest in the education and training of his grandson, particularly in the years immediately preceding his death. A programme of work in Swedish industry, commerce and agriculture was organised for the Crown Prince, and Carl Gustaf also spent much time abroad gaining experience of foreign affairs which now play an increasing part in the life of the monarch. He worked in London at the Swedish Embassy, the Swedish Chamber of Commerce and also at Hambro's Bank. In addition to this he was for a time in attendance on the Swedish delegation at the United Nations as well as working for the Swedish International Development Authority in Africa. His scope may be less wide than that of previous monarchs, but his training has prepared him thoroughly for the difficult part he will have to play.

The King's marriage in 1976 (the first occasion since 1797 that a reigning king was married in Sweden) attracted a great deal of pro-monarchical feeling and will be of enormous benefit to his office. The Queen, formerly Miss Silvia Sommerlath, was a successful career-girl whose good looks and manifest abilities have endeared her to the Swedish people. She is the daughter of a German businessman and was brought up in Germany and Brazil. She first met the King while working for the Organizing Committee for the Munich Olympic Games in 1972. They both enjoy skiing and he sails and hunts. They have one child, Princess Victoria, born on the 14th July 1977.

In a country as egalitarian as Sweden the job of the king is far from easy. Gustaf VI was a democrat and an intellectual and, in a society where educational achievement is held in high regard, was greatly loved and respected. Carl Gustaf has shown every promise of being as capable as his grandfather. He is keenly aware of the part he is to play which, judging from the longevity of Swedish kings, is likely to be a lengthy one, and his views are most clearly expressed in a motto he coined at his succession; 'For Sweden – in keeping with the times.'

Their Majesties King Carl Gustaf XVI and Queen Silvia.

King Carl Gustaf with his bride Queen Silvia turns to acknowledge the cheers from the crowds as they return to the royal palace from a boat ride in Stockholm. June 1976.

Below King Carl Gustaf helps his bride Queen Silvia into their coach after the wedding ceremony for a ceremonial drive through Stockholm.

Opposite above The marriage of Princess Christina to Mr Tord Magnusen in June 1974. A family group in the royal palace, Stockholm. From left to right – Mr John Ambler, Princess Margaretha, Princess Lillian, Crown Princess Beatrix of the Netherlands, Crown Princess Sonja of Norway,

Queen Ingrid of Denmark, Crown Prince Carl Gustaf (now King).

Opposite below Princess Christina with her bridegroom Mr Tord Magnusen poses with their pages and maids of honour on their wedding day in the royal palace, Stockholm.

Left Queen Silvia.

Opposite King Carl Gustaf and Queen Silvia attend the opera house in Stockholm.

Below Prince Carl Gustaf (now King) shares a table with Princess Grace of Monaco at the 25th Centenary celebrations of the Persian dynasty at Persepolis, Iran, in 1971.

Above Proud moment – Queen Silvia with Princess Victoria.

Right Queen Silvia with Princess Victoria, photographed in one of the lounges in the royal palace, Stockholm.

Opposite above left Mother and Baby – Queen Silvia with her daughter Princess Victoria at eight months, in the royal palace, Stockholm.

Opposite above right King Carl Gustaf and Queen Silvia with their baby daughter Princess Victoria.

Opposite below Queen Silvia takes the hand of her husband King Carl Gustaf in one of the lounges of the royal palace.

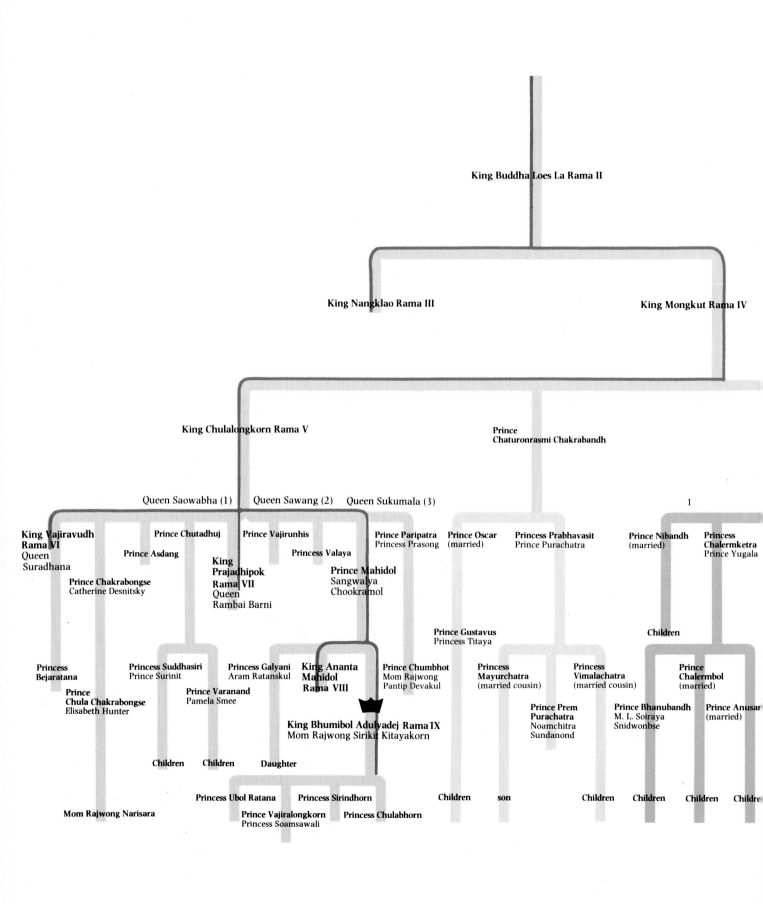

King Buddha Loes La Rama II

King Nangklao Rama III

King Mongkut Rama IV

King Chulalongkorn Rama V

Prince
Chaturonrasmi Chakrabandh

Queen Saowabha (1)   Queen Sawang (2)   Queen Sukumala (3)   1

**King Vajiravudh
Rama VI**
Queen
Suradhana

Prince Chutadhuj

Prince Vajirunhis

Prince Paripatra
Princess Prasong

Prince Oscar
(married)

Princess Prabhavasit
Prince Purachatra

Prince Nibandh
(married)

**Princess
Chalermketra**
Prince Yugala

Prince Asdang

Princess Valaya

Prince Chakrabongse
Catherine Desnitsky

**King
Prajadhipok
Rama VII**
Queen
Rambai Barni

Prince Mahidol
Sangwalya
Chookramol

Prince Gustavus
Princess Titaya

Children

Princess
Bejaratana

Princess Suddhasiri
Prince Surinit

Princess Galyani
Aram Ratanskul

**King Ananta
Mahidol
Rama VIII**

Prince Chumbhot
Mom Rajwong
Pantip Devakul

Princess
Mayurchatra
(married cousin)

Princess
Vimalachatra
(married cousin)

**Prince
Chalermbol**
(married)

Prince
Chula Chakrabongse
Elisabeth Hunter

Prince Varanand
Pamela Smee

King Bhumibol Adulyadej Rama IX
Mom Rajwong Sirikit Kitayakorn

**Prince Prem
Purachatra**
Noamchitra
Sundanond

Prince Bhanubandh
M. L. Soiraya
Snidwonbse

Prince Anusar
(married)

Children   Children   **Daughter**

Children   son

Children   Children   Children   Childre

Mom Rajwong Narisara

Princess Ubol Ratana

Princess Sirindhorn

Prince Vajiralongkorn
Princess Soamsawali

Princess Chulabhorn

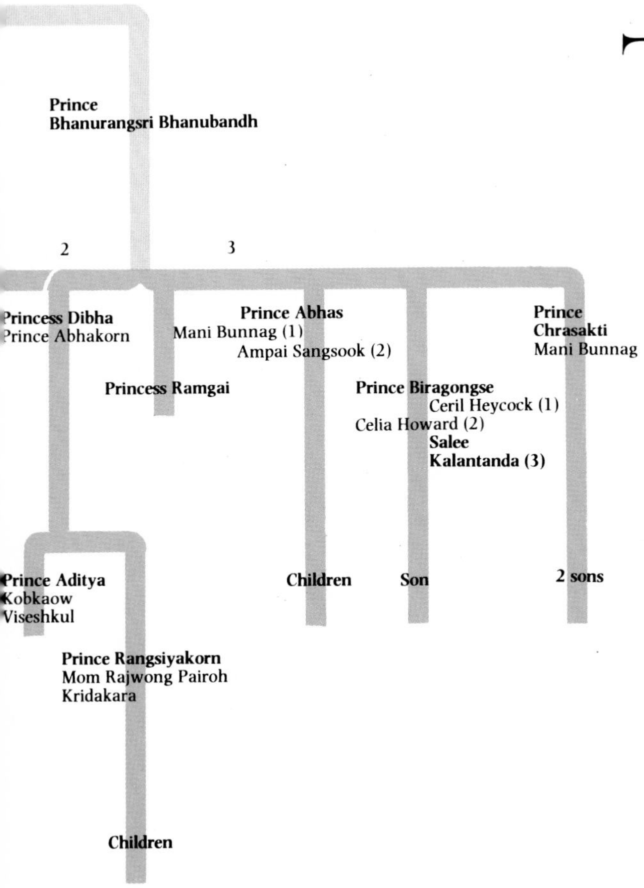

THAILAND
The House of Chakri

Prince
Bhanurangsri Bhanubandh

2

3

Princess Dibha
Prince Abhakorn

Prince Abhas
Mani Bunnag (1)
Ampai Sangsook (2)

Prince
Chrasakti
Mani Bunnag

Princess Ramgai

Prince Biragongse
Ceril Heycock (1)
Celia Howard (2)
Salee
Kalantanda (3)

Prince Aditya
Kobkaow
Viseshkul

Children

Son

2 sons

Prince Rangsiyakorn
Mom Rajwong Pairoh
Kridakara

Children

KING BHUMIBOL ADULYADEJ

The House of Chakri

King Bhumibol Adulyadej of Thailand is the ninth king of the Chakri dynasty, ruling over a country approximately the size of France. He was nineteen years old when he succeeded his brother in June 1946, and immediately after his accession to the throne, he returned to Switzerland to complete his education. In 1950 he returned home and married Sirikit, lovely daughter of His Highness Prince Chandaburi Suranath, who had been Thai Minister to France and Denmark, and Ambassador to Britain. His daughter had continued her schooling in all three countries. The coronation took place in 1950, the same year as the marriage.

Thailand is a beautiful country; it has also been very primitive. Successive rulers have worked steadily to improve conditions, but to a great degree the country remained feudal. Not until the accession of Chulalongkorn in 1868, was it permitted for those having audience with the King to sit or stand instead of crouching on hands and knees before him.

Devotion to the Buddhist faith has continued unbroken. As Defender of the Faith, the King appoints all religious high dignitaries and Bhumibol entered the priesthood for a period in 1956, leaving the palace to live with his fellow priests at Bovornives Temple, and his queen to act as Regent.

Under the constitution, the King is also Head of all the armed forces, but essentially a man of peace, his greatest desire is to keep his country out of war and to further the general welfare of his people. He was the first ruler in Thai history to visit the North-East province, an extremely poor, under-developed, long neglected area. Since then, he has constantly toured the country, learning at first hand of the problems and needs of his people. Education he sees as a means of bringing stability and progress, donating his own money to schools, personally presenting degrees to all graduating stu-

dents, and setting up a Foundation to award scholarships to those of outstanding ability to continue their studies abroad.

Public health is a matter of great concern to him, and he has given two mobile units to send teams of workers out into the provinces where there are no health centres or Red Cross Units. He has presented a motor-boat fully equipped as a medical unit to help care for inhabitants living on the canals and rivers, and started a fund for a clinic for the rehabilitation of those who had suffered polio in the 1952-53 epidemic. In the cholera epidemic six years later, he set up a similar fund to provide vaccination, medical treatment and monetary relief, and more of his own money has gone towards the training of personnel and research into leprosy. To the buildings his money provided, he gave the name *Raj Pracha Samasai* which means mutual support between King and people.

He is deeply interested in the development of agriculture and industry. Rice is the basis of the country's economy but, where the soil is not suitable, alternative products are recommended to the farmers. The King believes in encouraging local industries and is constantly visiting factories, promoting new ideas, talking to the people and striving to better conditions.

Queen Sirikit is equally tireless in her work for welfare and the Red Cross of which she is President. Both she and the King delight in their family of one son and three daughters – once referred to by their father as 'his four *Thaiphoons*'. Princess Ubol Ratana was born in April 1951, Prince Vajiralongkorn in July 1952, Princess Sirindhorn in April 1955, and Princess Chulabhorn in July 1957.

The best known to the people of all Thai rulers, Bhumibol and his Queen are almost certainly the best loved.

His Majesty King Bhumibol Adulyadej and
Her Majesty Queen Sirikit.

Below A brilliantly colourful scene as the King and Queen, shielded from the mid-day sun by huge umbrellas, say goodbye to VIP visitors at Chiengmai airport.

Above The King and Queen meet local people in Bangkok as a woman lies prostrate before the Queen, an Eastern sign of devotion.

Left A Toast to each other: Queen Sirikit of Thailand and Queen Elizabeth II at the State banquet in the Grand Palace, Bangkok, during the State visit to Thailand in 1972.

During a formal occasion in the
Grand Palace, Bangkok, the Queen
directs a warm glance at her
husband, King Bhumibol.

Crown Prince Vajiralongkorn in
full military dress with his wife
Princess Soamsawali in their own
palace in Bangkok.

Above Queen Sirikit in formal pose.

Above right Her Majesty wearing a large straw hat and Chinese-style costume as she poses in the grounds of Bhuping Palace.

Right King Bhumibol, an ardent photographer taking photographs of his wife Queen Sirikit on the terrace of Bhuping Palace at Chiengmai in northern Thailand.

Opposite A beautiful setting in the cool of the evening in the grounds of Bhuping Palace.

Above Crown Prince Vajiralongkorn with his wife Princess
Soamsawali in a very informal
setting at the Ambhara Palace,
Bangkok.

Right Queen Sirikit on the terrace
of Chiengmai's Bhuping Palace
with the tea pavilion in the
background. She possesses a
warmth and charm which makes
her a joy to photograph.

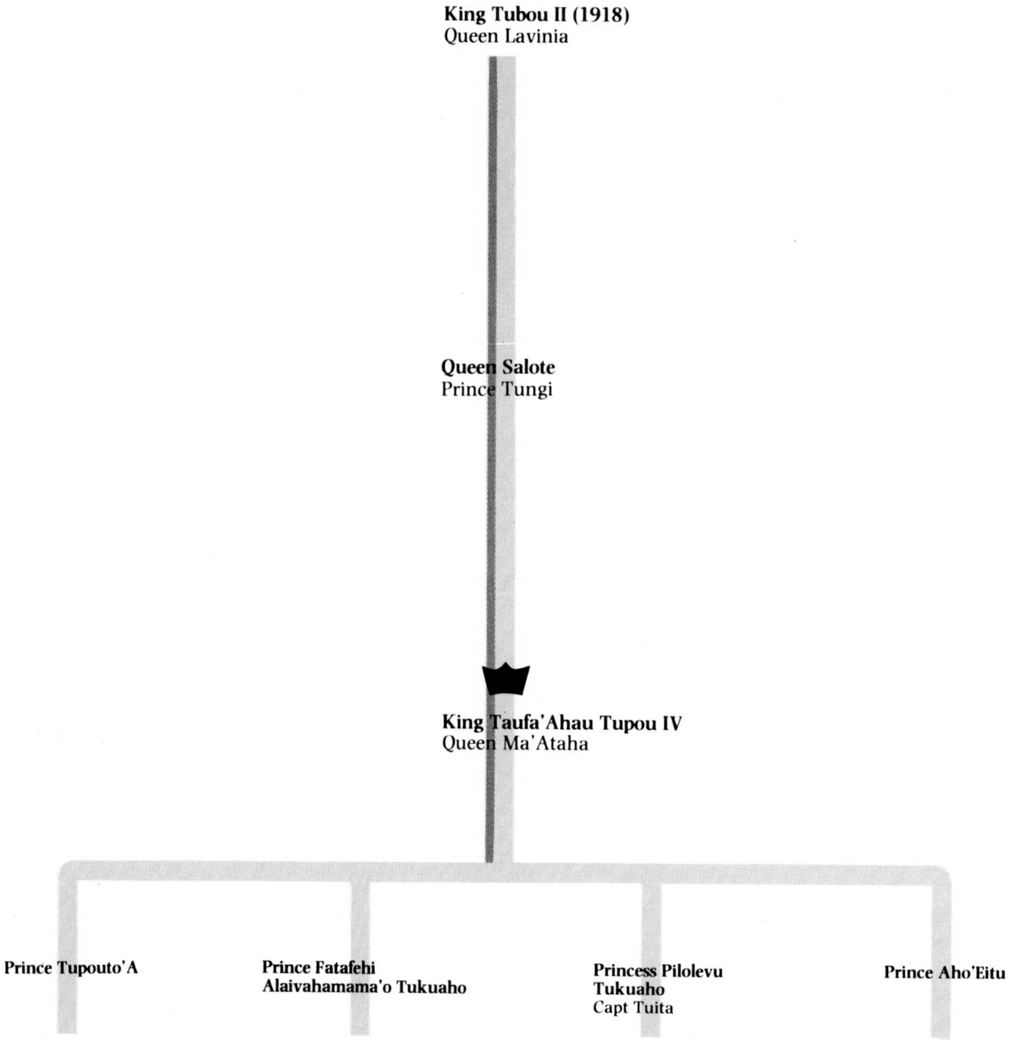

King Tubou II (1918)
Queen Lavinia

Queen Salote
Prince Tungi

King Taufa'Ahau Tupou IV
Queen Ma'Ataha

Prince Tupouto'A

Prince Fatafehi
Alaivahamama'o Tukuaho

Princess Pilolevu
Tukuaho
Capt Tuita

Prince Aho'Eitu

TONGA
The House of Kanokupolu

KING TAUFA'AHAU TUPOU IV

House of Kanokupolu

Tonga is the last remaining Polynesian kingdom and archaeologists say that the islands have been settled since the fifth century B.C. Tongatapu, the largest island of the archipelago, was discovered by Tasman in 1643 and since that date the islands have had close links with Europe, and particularly with Great Britain which concluded the first of many 'Treaties of Friendship' with Tonga in 1879.

The first Englishman seriously to study the islands was Captain Cook who visited the archipelago in 1773 in his ship the *Endeavour*. The famous tortoise 'Tu'i Malila' that lived in the grounds of the royal palace and died in 1966 was reputedly left behind by him. Cook named the group the 'Friendly Islands' after the courtesy of the islanders, a characteristic that the Tongans are noted for even today, the national toast 'ota atu' meaning 'love, luck and good feelings to you'.

A less happy visit was that made by Captain Bligh in 1789 after the *Bounty* mutiny. Eight years after this the first Christian Missionaries reached the Friendly Islands. These early missions were not a success and it was not until the arrival of Walter Lawry of the Wesleyan Missionary Society in 1822 that Christianity achieved any foothold. Methodism has played an important part in the development of Tonga, King Taufa'Ahau I being one of the first converts and beginning a tradition of Methodism in the royal house that continues even today.

Taufa'Ahau was the first of Tonga's chiefs to unite the islands by conquest. He was six foot six inches tall, an impressive figure in every way, and he proved to be an enlightened and benevolent ruler, giving Tonga representative government.

In 1845 he founded the present royal dynasty, being formally proclaimed King George Tupou I after King George III, his wife taking the name Salote after Queen Charlotte.

The present King, Taufa'Ahau Tupou IV, is the great-great-great-grandson of George Tupou I. He was born on 4th July 1918 and succeeded his mother Queen Salote on her death in 1965. Queen Salote was a popular figure in Great Britain, winning the hearts of the British people by driving through London in an open carriage at Queen Elizabeth's coronation in 1953, apparently oblivious of the pouring rain.

The King was educated locally in Tonga and at Newington University in Australia. He was married in June 1947. He and his wife have four children; Crown Prince Tupouto'A being born on 4th May 1948, Princess Pilolevu on 14th November 1951, Prince Fatafehi Alaivahamama'O Tukuaho on 17th December 1954 and Prince Aho'Eitu on 12th July 1959. Princess Pilolevu was married in June 1976 to Captain Tuita, a member of the nobility and a second cousin of the Princess.

Tonga is a constitutional monarchy, the Constitution of 1875 providing for a government consisting of the Sovereign, a Privy Council and Cabinet, a Legislative Assembly and a Judiciary. There is a happy mixture of the old and new in Tongan society; Nuku'alofa, the capital, boasting much European influence while the countryside shows little change from the days of Taufa'Ahau I. The economy is mainly agricultural and the King devotes a large amount of time to supervising and encouraging advancement in farming methods.

His Majesty King Taufa'Ahau Tupou IV.

King Taufa'Ahau escorts Queen
Elizabeth whilst Queen Ma'Ataha
escorts Prince Philip through
singing and clapping Tongan girls
during a day's visit to the Island.

158

Right King Taufa'Ahau in full dress military uniform in the grounds of his palace at Nuku'Alofa.

Below right The King and Queen of Tonga.